VOLUNTEER PROGRAM
ADMINISTRATION

A Handbook for Museums and Other Cultural Institutions

Joan Kuyper
in collaboration with
Ellen Cochran Hirzy and
Kathleen Huftalen

aca BOOKS

AMERICAN COUNCIL FOR THE ARTS
in association with
AMERICAN ASSOCIATION FOR MUSEUM
VOLUNTEERS

Published by the American Council for the Arts, One East 53rd Street, New York, NY 10022.

Director of Publishing: Robert Porter
Book design by Kingsley Parker, Design Oasis

Library of Congress Cataloging-in-Publication Data
Kuyper, Joan
Volunteer program administration : a handbook for museums and other cultural organizations / Joan Kuyper ; with Ellen Hirzy and Kathleen Huftalen.
    p. cm.
Includes bibliographical references.
ISBN 0-915400-95-2 (pbk.)
1. Volunteer workers in museums—United
States—Management—Handbooks, manuals, etc. 2. Museums—United
States—Management—Handbooks, manuals, etc. I. Hirzy Ellen Cochran.
II. Huftalen, Kathleen R. III. Title.
AM11.K88   1993
069'.5'0973—dc20   93-8177
                             CIP

This publication was made possible
by the generous support of the
MARPAT Foundation

C O N T E N T S

LIST OF FIGURES

F o r e w o r d

Since its founding in 1976, the American Association for Museum Volunteers has had as its goals to promote professional standards for museum volunteers, provide a forum for exchange of ideas and information, and encourage volunteers and volunteer administrators to become familiar with volunteer projects and programs, locally and nationally. Publication of a handbook has long been seen as an appropriate way to make available to museum volunteer leaders the resources that will enable them to respond to the challenges intrinsic to volunteer program management in the 1990s.

As museums work to expand their public dimension, the trained volunteer and the efficiently administered volunteer program become increasingly central to helping the museum become the common ground where diverse populations can meet. Effective volunteer programs create cheerful ambassadors who make that common ground a welcoming and friendly place for the museum's community. Innovative and efficient recruitment programs invite that community to participate in the life of the institution. The consistent themes of this handbook are the importance of adequate training for volunteers, for volunteer administra-

tors, and for museum staff who work with volunteers, with the same consideration given to the administration of the museum's volunteer programs as is dedicated to other employee practices.

Volunteer Program Administration: A Handbook for Museums and Other Cultural Institutions could not have been completed without the many individuals who contributed their expertise toward ensuring that the material it contains reflects a cross-section of cultural institutions, from those museums whose volunteers number in the thousands to those that have a staff of three, every one a volunteer. The AAMV is grateful for the help given by Susan Ellis, Jane Glaser, Janice Majewski, Joanne Patton, Mary Grace Potter, Alan Ullberg, and Patricia E. Williams. The members of the AAMV Board of Directors who have served as continuing consultants are Mitzi Bhavnani, Sarah Brophy, Jean Eichelberger, Marilyn Hayden, Joan Larson, Cynthia Pinkston, Patricia Sands, Verdalee Tombelaine, and Wreatha Witte. Most important, Betty Jane Gerber's vision and continuing dedication to turning an idea into reality has enabled the material in this handbook to find its way to publication.

The programs and practices highlighted in *Volunteer Program Administration* illustrate just a few of the ways in which elected, appointed, or salaried museum volunteer program administrators have utilized management skills and organizational strategies to further the missions of their institutions. The AAMV hopes that this handbook enables a sharing of some of the incredible wealth of talent, innovation, and dedication with which volunteer programs have so greatly enriched America's museums.

Marian Nielsen
President, American Association for Museum Volunteers

Preface

In 1986, as a past president of the American Association for Museum Volunteers (AAMV), a board member of the American Association of Museums (AAM), and a museum trustee, I was asked to participate in a roundtable discussion on volunteerism and trusteeship in the arts involving Milton Rhodes, president of the American Council for the Arts (ACA), and others. The proceedings of that meeting were published in the summer 1987 issue of the *Journal of Arts Management and Law*. The organizer and editor of that opus was Joan Kuyper. At the conclusion of that endeavor, Milton, Joan, and I agreed that a handbook focused on the complex and fascinating world of the museum volunteer was long overdue. Armed with this conviction, we quickly recruited AAM executive director Edward H. Able and deputy executive director Kathy Dwyer Southern, and a partnership among the AAMV, the AAM, and the ACA was formed to bring this project to fruition.

Special mention should be made of the outstanding leadership of Marian Nielsen, who was president of the AAMV during the production period of this manuscript. It is an effort that reflects the extraordinary contributions of our publisher at the ACA, Robert Porter, and

three special people. In collaboration with Joan Kuyper, Ellen Cochran Hirzy and Kathleen Huftalen have researched, produced, polished, and enriched the text and resource section to deliver a product that demonstrates a high standard of professional excellence.

This handbook would not have become a reality, however, without the inspired leadership and support of Mrs. Jefferson Patterson, whose accomplishments and interests have earned her the AAMV's Museum Volunteer of the Year Award, an honor she shares with Mrs. George Bush. Marvin Breckinridge Patterson served for many years on the AAMV Board and has been on the Advisory Board for several more. Taking on the diverse roles of founder, trustee, donor, and volunteer, she has had a major impact on the general welfare of a number of cultural and educational institutions. Her interests are substantial, broad, and personal, and the AAMV is honored to be included among them. In 1928, she joined the Frontier Nursing Service as a courier and eventually became chairman of its Board of Governors. More recently, Jefferson Patterson Park and Museum, Bowdoin College, the Corcoran Gallery of Art, the Textile Museum, the Smithsonian Institution, the

Calvert Marine Museum, the Folger Shakespeare Library, and the Historical Society of Washington, D.C., are just a few institutions that have benefited from her time and interest. Her generous donation from the MARPAT Foundation has made this handbook possible, and it is with deep gratitude that we dedicate this work to her.

The oath of the Athenian citizen states that "we will unceasingly seek to quicken the sense of public duty. . . . We will transmit this city not only not less but greater, better, and more beautiful than it was transmitted to us." Mrs. Patterson is indeed a treasured citizen of America's cultural world, which will be transmitted to the future greater, better, and more beautiful because of her contributions.

Betty Jane Johnson Gerber
Chairman, Museum Volunteer
Handbook Project
American Association for Museum
Volunteers

Introduction

♦ On the floor of a science-technology museum, a retired scientist talks with a family about gravity, his voice sparkling with the accumulated wisdom and enthusiasm of a lifetime of experience.

♦ At the information desk of a large urban art museum, volunteers offer a warm welcome—supplemented by directions to the latest exhibition and the museum's restaurant—to a group of visitors.

♦ At an outdoor history museum, a volunteer interpreter in eighteenth-century dress transports visiting high school students to a time when life may not have been as simple as it seemed.

♦ In the registrar's office of a natural history museum, a volunteer helps with the time-consuming task of entering detailed information about the specimens in the museum's collection into a database.

These are just a few of the ways in which volunteers enrich the many activities of the nation's museums. According to a recent survey by the American Asso-

ciation of Museums, more than 370,000 volunteers work in museums in the United States. In the words of Paul N. Perrot, director of the Santa Barbara Museum of Art, volunteers "represent a *personal commitment* to the ideals of the institution. . . . They can be called precious assets, in the broadest sense of the word."

About This Handbook

This book is intended for a diverse audience: museum volunteers, both experienced and new; volunteer program administrators; paid staff who supervise volunteers; elected and appointed volunteer program officers and leaders; and, last but not least, museum directors and trustees. Readers in museums and cultural institutions of all sizes and types—from small historic sites to encyclopedic natural history museums, from community art centers to zoos, from youth museums to botanical gardens—will find useful information in the following pages.

Museum volunteer programs are as varied in size, structure, and focus as are museums themselves, so clearly this handbook cannot be all things to all people. It offers guidelines and options for volunteer program administration—not hard-and-fast rules or a blueprint, but an approach that can be adapted depending on the needs of the individual institution. The seven chapters are supplemented by a Resource and Networking Guide that will enable readers to tailor the suggestions in the handbook even further to fit their own needs.

A common thread of all volunteer programs—and all museums—is public service. Regardless of size, structure, or history, every museum volunteer program is a people-to-people effort. Effective program administration that supports the institution's mission while creating a rewarding professional atmosphere for the individual volunteer is a solid foundation for the service museums provide.

1

A VITAL RESOURCE

VOLUNTEERS AND
MUSEUMS

Volunteers are an integral part of the rich mosaic of museums in the United States. In museums of all sizes and types, in all regions of the country, volunteers join in partnership with trustees and paid staff to carry out the mission of their institutions. That mission centers on service to the public, and service is the essence of volunteering in museums.

Today, the concept of volunteering as public service has great currency. *Excellence and Equity: Education and the Public Dimension of Museums,* a report issued in 1992 by the American Associa-

tion of Museums (AAM), asserts that "every area of museum activity contributes to . . . the important public service museums provide."[1] In the same vein, the AAM adopted a new code of ethics for museums in 1991, "informed by a renewed emphasis on the historic American concepts of museums as public trusts and museum work as service to society."[2] As museums face the growing social and economic challenges of our complex global society, they are underscoring their commitment to the many aspects of their public dimension.

The Value of Volunteers

A recent study by the American Association of Museums indicates that more than 375,000 volunteers serve America's museums.[3] Volunteers make essential and widely recognized contributions to museums' public dimension. They help transform the educational potential of their institutions into reality for visitors. They are a link between museums and their communities, bringing the voice of the community into the museum and representing the museum among its audiences. They help to generate significant financial support. They work as a team with paid staff, and they help to create programming that would not otherwise exist.

Many museums owe their existence to groups of interested volunteers who crafted a mission and purpose for the institution, formed the first board of trustees, and then administered the museum's operations until a paid staff was hired. Thousands of museums in the United States are run wholly by volunteers. Volunteers serve on the governing body, administer day-to-day operations, create and design exhibitions, conduct tours for visitors, produce publications, care for the collections, and maintain the building and grounds.

The skills and talents of volunteers are evident first and foremost in a museum's board of trustees. Trustees contribute considerable time and expertise to the governance of their institutions, and they assume significant legal obligations when they agree to take on the responsibilities of board members.

Beyond the board room, volunteers—gallery guides or information desk volunteers, for example—work directly with visitors. Others are involved in less visible but equally valuable service behind the scenes in administrative offices, libraries, and conservation laboratories. Volunteer efforts can be concentrated in one or more of five areas: public programs, visitor services, behind-the-scenes activities, fund raising and special events, and community relations.

Public Programs

Museum programs for the public encompass a range of themes and formats designed to engage visitors of all ages, interests, and backgrounds in the learning experience that museums offer. These programs include interpretive programs for all visitors, programs for schoolchildren and teachers, and programs for nontraditional audiences.

Interpretive Programs

A major activity of museum volunteers is the interpretation of collections and exhibitions for individual visitors or groups of visitors. Volunteers who specialize in interpretive programs may be called docents, interpreters, guides, or explainers, or they may have other titles. But each is involved in enhancing visitors' knowledge and understanding of the objects in the museum's collections and stimulating visitors to consider the ideas those objects represent.

Museums offer a variety of interpretive programs, usually planned by the education or curatorial departments, by a team of educators and curators, or by paid and volunteer staff together. Highlights tours that provide an overview of a museum's collections and programs are led by volunteers who have a thorough general knowledge of the museum. Thematic programs that concentrate on a particular aspect of the museum's collection or discipline—such as an artistic style, historic period, or scientific concept—usually appeal to visitors with specialized interests or knowledge and require volunteers with advanced subject-matter training and expertise in the subject matter. Tours of permanent or temporary exhibitions have a similar concentrated focus, but they often are designed for visitors with general interests. Some museums have "discovery rooms" or other participatory activities for families and children in which volunteers help visitors learn firsthand about concepts and objects.

Volunteers with special expertise can give museum lectures, teach classes, or present demonstrations. A historian can speak on the Underground Railroad as part of a history museum's Civil War lecture series. In a botanical garden, a master gardener can give lectures, administer plant clinics, provide consultations, and answer plant hotlines.

Interpretive programs require of the volunteer strong commitment and extensive training tailored to the program; the training may last a year or more. Volunteers who participate in such programs should be deeply interested in learning and willing to study the subject matter in some depth. They need excellent communication and teaching skills so that they can present the material effectively and enthusiastically. Flexibility is essential; they must be able to adapt to changing exhibits and subject matter and interact with visitors who have different backgrounds, interests, and learning styles. Because museums provide extensive training to volunteers working in interpretive programs, some require a contract with the volunteer for a specified period of service after, and in return for, the provision of training.

School Programs

Volunteers are important participants in the museum-school partnership, which has long been a hallmark of museum education. Museums reach school audiences not only through the traditional field trip. They offer programs for schoolchildren held in the museum and in the classroom; provide training and materials for teachers; and develop other activities, often in collaboration with schools, that join museum resources with the school curriculum. Volunteers may be involved in any of these programs. At the Asian Art Museum of San Francisco, for example, docents were involved in planning and conducting the Extended School Program, which follows the California state curriculum guidelines for the elementary, middle, and high school levels. At other museums, volunteers lead gallery tours for students or for teachers during teacher training workshops, present classroom programs that prepare students for museum visits, conduct participatory activities or special demonstrations, and help museum educators evaluate the effectiveness of museum-school programs.

Programs for Nontraditional Audiences

More and more museums are designing programs for people who have not typically participated in the institution. These audiences are highly diverse and may include senior citizens, high school students, disabled visitors, and people from a variety of ethnic and cultural backgrounds. Traditionally called "outreach" efforts because they once entailed taking special programs to groups in the community, these programs are now more directed at welcoming people of all ages, interests, backgrounds, and abilities into the museum. Programs designed to attract nontraditional audiences are often held in conjunction with exhibitions and involve volunteers who share the visitors background or interests. The Oakland Museum, for example, recruited guides from the diverse local community during "I Dream a World," an exhibition of photographs by African-American women, and "Strength and Diversity: Japanese-American Women 1885-1900." Other efforts are incorporated into ongoing educational programs. In Houston, the Children's Museum and the Junior League cosponsored the Overnight Adventure program for economically disadvantaged girls from seven to nine years old. The girls spend the night exploring

the museum. As a link between the museum and the community, volunteers can offer special insights into the audiences the museum could serve and ways to assure that all programs and activities help these visitors feel part of the museum.

Other Public Programs

Many museums become true cultural centers in their communities, providing space for a variety of programs. Some museums present music, theater, dance, and film as part of their programming. Outdoor festivals sponsored by a city's cultural institutions mark a holiday or a milestone in local history, welcome the arrival of seasons, or showcase local talent. Events concentrated in a neighborhood promote the offerings of nearby museums. In New York City, the Morris Jumel Mansion, a historic house, began an herb garden to involve more local people and opened the museum for weddings and community events to attract the museum's neighbors in Harlem. Historic sites take advantage of seasonal events such as sheep-shearing or harvest time to present special programs. Volunteers are always active in these programs, which require extensive planning, complicated logistics, and an expanded work force. Sometimes these programs are the sole responsibility of volunteers.

Visitor Services

The museum experience is shaped by more than exhibitions and interpretive programs. The way in which people are

FIGURE 1.1

Programs for Nontraditional Audiences

A Ray of Hope for Philadelphia Homeless Children

More than ninety volunteers—students, members of the business community, and people who were once homeless themselves—were the backbone of an unusual cultural and literacy program developed by the Museum at Drexel University for children and mothers living in homeless shelters in west Philadelphia. The goal of the Saturday afternoon program was to offer interactive, noncompetitive, and nonacademic activities that bolstered the children's self-esteem, gave them a chance to experience success, and let them know that people cared about them. Ultimately, the program's creators hoped the children would take away a greater sense of empowerment, self-worth, and respect for others.

Volunteers attended an orientation session that combined nuts and bolts with program philosophy. Volunteers learned how to guide the children in the program's rich mix of activities, which included hands-on creative art experiences, performing artists, a computer literacy component for the mothers, and visits to local cultural institutions. Orientation also explained the program's core principles, which stressed empowerment and self-esteem, and gave techniques for interacting with children who suffer from the hopelessness and uncertainty of shelter existence. Volunteers worked directly with the children and their mothers during the three-hour program and then participated in program evaluation at the close of the day.

During the program, volunteers helped the children explore alternatives and use their imagination. By making connections between the activities and everyday life, they encouraged the youngsters to see that they are worthwhile individuals who have options they can exercise. For many homeless children, the program was their first experience with a museum. With the involvement of caring volunteers who focused attention on the children's needs, the experience was all the more valuable.

Due to a financial crisis at Drexel University, the museum closed in July 1991. The program was temporarily held at the Museum for Archeology and Anthropology of the University of Pennsylvania, but is no longer operating. Jean Henry, former director of the museum, can provide information about starting a program for homeless children. A videotape about the Drexel program is also available.

Jean Henry
1810 Rittenhouse Square
Philadelphia, PA 19103
(215) 893-0706

welcomed to the museum, the availability of services and amenities, and the attitudes of volunteers and staff are significant factors. The visitor services that volunteers provide help to create an environment conducive to positive visitor experiences.

Information Services

Volunteers at information desks are usually the first contact visitors have with the museum. These volunteers must be prepared to meet and welcome a diverse public and respond to their needs and interests. Visitors will inquire not only about museum exhibits, programs, and amenities—such as food services and rest rooms—but also about bus schedules, other places of interest, and almost any imaginable topic related to the area in which the museum is located.

Museum Stores and Membership Services

Many museums depend on assistance from volunteers in museum stores and at membership sales desks; sometimes these operations are administered and staffed solely by volunteers. Typical jobs assigned to volunteers are buying, selling, pricing, receiving, and displaying merchandise; managing financial operations; and developing new products. Volunteers who work at membership sales desks answer questions about membership benefits and promote museum memberships to visitors.

Food Services

Some museums have volunteer-managed food services, with volunteers preparing and serving coffee, snacks, and lunches. Typical of these operations is the Garden Café at the Honolulu Academy of Arts, which is staffed by volunteers and open four days a week. Historic houses may have catering operations run by volunteers for weddings, community meetings, and other events. Other museums provide food for community events cosponsored by the museum, with volunteers demonstrating food preparation techniques and selling food to the public.

Behind-the-Scenes Activities

Many members of the public are unaware of the complex infrastructure in the museums they enjoy visiting. Work in the offices and laboratories of the museum offers stimulating and productive volunteer opportunities.

Collections and Exhibitions

Collections management, collections care, and exhibition preparation and maintenance are three areas in which volunteers provide behind-the-scenes assistance (see Figure 1.2). Technical support by skilled volunteers ranges from entering collections information into a computerized data base to creating labels and signage for exhibitions. In botanical gardens, aquariums, and zoos, volunteers maintain exhibits and feed and care for animals. Small institutions in particular often depend on volunteers to support staff in cataloging collections, designing and constructing exhibitions, and carrying out routine conservation work. Frequently, graduate students in the museum's discipline, retired professionals, and others with special expertise fill these positions. In larger museums as well, including the many museums of the Smithsonian, professionals work behind the scenes as volunteer scholars, technicians, and scientists.

Libraries and Archives

Museum libraries and archives utilize many volunteer skills. Volunteers index books, photographs, documents, pamphlets, and archival collections. They enter information into computerized data bases; prepare information for files; and process, sort, and prepare manuscripts, newspapers, and other collections material. Volunteers also translate documents and periodicals into English, summarize and report on library materials, and work on conservation projects. The American Museum of Natural History has a special archives team that works under staff archivists. Led and staffed by volunteers, the team has assisted in many projects over the years, including the organization of archival holdings that had been stored in the basement of the Hayden Planetarium.

Research

Volunteers can contribute to the research that is a fundamental activity in most museums (see Figures 1.2, 1.3). This work includes both research on a part of the collection or a specific subject area in the museum's discipline and research conducted in conjunction with exhibitions and publications. Volunteers in some museums carry out research for exhibition catalogues and prepare background information for interpretive programs. Some volunteers undertake the planning of their own research projects.

Volunteers also work with paid staff to edit manuscripts, proofread galleys, or prepare indexes. In botanical gardens, zoos, and arboretums, volunteers help horticulturists, landscape historians, and wildlife specialists do research; some identify specimens and prepare them for permanent collections; and some even do independent field research with plants and animals.

Administrative Offices

Volunteers support the objectives of a museum's various departments by providing behind-the-scenes assistance in administrative offices. The public relations, development, membership, education, and finance departments of a museum can benefit from the skills of volunteers who prepare press materials, compile reports, respond to telephone inquiries, help with tour scheduling, and provide routine administrative assistance. Museum educators who are conducting visitor research often train volunteers to assist with collecting, compiling, and analyzing data.

Executive Management

Corporate executives volunteer their services in marketing, sales, financial management, and legal matters, as well as on boards of trustees. Often the prerequisite to funding for the museum from a corporation, these volunteer placements usually are determined by top museum administration and last only a short time. Organizations such as Business Volunteers for the Arts and Volunteer Lawyers

FIGURE
1.2

Behind the Scenes

Preserving Southern California History

At a southern California historic site, volunteers have made a visible difference in two vital behind-the-scenes activities: collections care and research. The Workman and Temple Family Homestead Museum, which opened in 1981, is a six-acre site in City of Industry that documents nearly ninety years of the region's history and culture. Owned and maintained by the city, the Homestead includes two historic houses—an adobe home built in the 1840s and remodeled in the 1870s, and a Spanish Colonial Revival residence built between 1919 and 1925.

The environment in the museum's buildings, like those in most historic houses, is difficult to control. Humidity and temperature fluctuate, light levels change, dust is pervasive, and pests are a problem. As the museum's collections grew, so did conservation needs, and by 1985 the time and skills of the museum's paid staff and independent conservators were stretched to the limit. The solution was to create a volunteer textile and costume conservation group. The concept was so successful that talented and enthusiastic volunteers now work with other parts of the collections.

The first volunteers vacuum-cleaned every textile item on display in La Casa Nueva, the museum's 1920s period home. They went on to repair beadwork on 1920s dresses, devise furniture vacuuming screens from fiberglass window screening, and figure out how to wet-clean textiles in a second-floor conservation laboratory that has no running water. Now volunteers do all kinds of routine collec-

tions care and maintenance, from dusting books to cleaning metal objects to cleaning and repairing items in the museum's large collection of 1920s sheet music.

The extensive research that is the foundation of collections documentation and interpretation in all museums has been especially important to the Homestead, which is a relatively young institution. Ongoing research enables paid staff and volunteers to develop the documentation necessary to restore buildings, identify artifacts, and interpret the history of the site and its inhabitants. Research is part of volunteer training; the subjects volunteers have explored include household linens of the 1920s, early kitchen appliances, and the first settlers' efforts to live off the land. The products of volunteers' research efforts are evident throughout the site—in the authenticity of the period settings, the docents' vivid portrayals of life on the homestead and the smaller, changing, interpretive exhibits.

Visitors to the Workman and Temple Family Homestead Museum reap the true benefits of the volunteers' behind-the-scenes collections care and research efforts. They enjoy a rewarding and illuminating glimpse of the social history, art, and architecture of southern California during the 1840s, 1870s and 1920s.

Workman and Temple
Family Homestead Museum
15415 East Don Julian Road
City of Industry, CA 91744
(818) 968-8492

for the Arts also provide volunteer assistance. Such volunteer projects are clearly defined with specific goals and a set timetable. Although the museum may have to pay certain administrative costs, the results can justify an added overhead expense. Sometimes corporate executive involvement will expand to provision of printing, survey design, or the use of telephones for fund raising.

Building and Grounds

Volunteers assist with the beautification of museums indoors and out. Many museums, large and small, have committees of volunteers who provide flowers and design arrangements for galleries and reception areas. Sometimes funded by a benefactor or by the museum guild or members' organization, these services make the museum attractive not only for openings and special events but also throughout the year. Volunteers can be responsible for the maintenance of the museum grounds. Groups of volunteers plan, plant, and maintain gardens and design and construct displays. In smaller museums, volunteers' contribution to building maintenance (mostly minor repairs), cleaning of collection objects and rooms, and painting often compensates for budgetary restraints. Museums can train volunteers to serve as gallery security assistants under the supervision of museum guards, although in some institutions union contracts may prohibit such a practice.

Fund Raising and Special Events

The financial support that volunteers provide museums through guilds and "friends" groups is a critical element of museum budgets. This support comes not only as monetary contributions, but in the form of new museum members and new volunteers, and thus new advocates for the museum. Membership in some volunteer fund-raising groups is by invitation; others are open to anyone who wishes to join. They exist in a variety of forms, even within a single institution: women's and men's councils, business volunteers, "young friends," and special-interest groups that support particular galleries or collections. Organizations of younger supporters are especially popular today; the Virginia Museum, the Phillips Collection, and the South Street Seaport Museum are just a few of the museums that have created such groups.

Fund-raising groups usually work with the development department. They sponsor special events for museum exhibition openings; contribute time and support for holiday celebrations, outdoor festivals, and performing arts presentations; sponsor lectures and special study programs; and conduct tours for museum members related to the museum's collections or subject area.

FIGURE 1.3

The Ecomuseum
New Volunteer Opportunities

An expanded museum concept, the *ecomuseum*, is emerging that offers great potential for involving volunteers. In an ecomuseum, the "collection" encompasses everything about the past, present, and future heritage that makes a region unique—including buildings, topographical features, flora and fauna. The people who live in and visit the ecomuseum are educated and entertained by it and thus made more aware of its value.

In Washington, D.C., the Georgetown Heritage Trust is developing this concept in the Georgetown Historic District, and volunteers are playing a key role. As part of its mission to enhance the interpretation of Georgetown's history, the organization has begun an ambitious project to transform the district into an ecomuseum. Although Georgetown has been officially recognized as a historic district since 1950, no survey of its historic resources has ever been conducted. The Georgetown Heritage Trust's first step—with the energetic involvement of volunteers—is to compile and computerize critical information on Georgetown's cultural resources for the historical record. Research and sur-

vey work in this important early phase of the ecomuseum are being conducted by volunteer and paid professionals and by trained lay volunteers. Volunteer researchers are helping to compile and analyze existing data on the area; conducting on-site surveys of the physical attributes of historic structures; seeking information to establish dates for undocumented buildings; and assisting with data entry. The volunteers are residents of the historic district, students from several universities in the area, members of the Business and Professional Association of Georgetown, and friends and advisors of the Georgetown Heritage Trust.

As the ecomuseum continues to evolve in Georgetown, volunteers will continue as active partners in the effort to document, preserve, and interpret the area's historic and cultural resources.

Georgetown Heritage Trust
Betty Jane Gerber, President
Halcyon House
3400 Prospect Street NW
Washington, DC 20007
(202) 338-0731

Community Relations

Volunteers provide much more than enthusiastic service within the museum's walls. They are a vital link between the museum and its community. They help bring the museum into the community in the form of special programs, involvement with civic organizations, and contact with community leaders, and they bring the community into the museum by working to expand the museum's audience and increase the number of volunteers. Most museums ask their volunteers to use their extensive community contacts to help expand and strengthen the institution's base of support.

Much involvement by museum volunteers in community relations is informal. Simply by being active citizens, volunteers can carry the museum's message to others. Membership in other organizations, professional interests, social contacts, and family activities all present opportunities for making the museum known and inviting broader community participation.

Formal community relations activities include speakers' bureaus that send volunteers to speak to organizations about the museum's collection and programs and about volunteer opportunities. Such presentations can be designed to stimulate greater participation in the museum; some speakers' bureaus target segments of the community not typically served by the museum in order to attract new audiences. They can also generate an interest in volunteering, especially if the presentation focuses on a topic related to the audience's interests. The most effective presentations are made by volunteers who are connected in some way to the organization being addressed.

Volunteers also serve in a public affairs and advocacy capacity by representing the museum in various situations or at selected community functions. When the museum needs a spokesperson to testify before a legislative body in its behalf, skilled volunteers can have a strong impact. Volunteers make excellent advocates, especially in times of crisis, by speaking for or against proposed legislation, lobbying against possible reductions in support for the museum, or raising the public's consciousness through praise for the museum's contributions to community life.

Active volunteer involvement in community relations is absolutely critical to the effectiveness of a museum's public service. The hours that volunteers contribute to public programs, visitor services, behind-the-scenes activities, fund raising, and special events have even greater purpose and meaning when they are supported by a concerted effort to engage the museum in the community it serves.

2
LAYING THE GROUNDWORK

THE VOLUNTEER PROGRAM'S MISSION AND STRUCTURE

Successful museum volunteer programs share three characteristics: a planning process that articulates the program's mission, goals, and objectives; a sound base of support from the museum's board and administration; and a structure appropriate to the institution, the program, and the audience. Whether the museum is a small community institution with no paid staff or a large urban institution with a complex organizational structure, these characteristics are the foundation for a viable, self-perpetuating volunteer program that is focused on serving the museum's audience.

Developing a Long-Range Plan

Mission-driven long-range planning is the first step in creating or restructuring a volunteer program. A periodic review of mission, goals, and objectives is also an essential planning tool and a source of renewal and revitalization for an existing program. The museum's mission statement is the starting point, because volunteer activities must be focused on fulfilling the vision it expresses.

Planning for a new program has the obvious benefit of providing a carefully thought-out foundation for a volunteer effort that is coordinated with the mission of the institution. New programs should devote adequate time to planning to assure that before the first volunteer is recruited, the mission, goals, objectives, and procedures are in place. A program without a sound foundation will not attract and stimulate committed volunteers and consequently will not serve the museum as it is intended to do.

An existing program also has much to gain from periodic planning exercises. A program may need restructuring, as when several independent volunteer entities are consolidated. A reevaluation of volunteer activities might be called for in light of changing audience demographics, new museum programs, a changing financial situation, or the availability of volunteers in the community. Whether planning leads to reaffirming the program's purposes or rethinking and revising those purposes, it is vital to the health of the volunteer program.

The planning process for establishing or revitalizing a volunteer program involves the following steps:

1. Determine procedures. Establish a planning committee, decide on the steps in the process, define expectations, and set a timetable. The committee may include volunteers involved in each of the types of activity described in chapter 1; board members with volunteer experience; key staff members who currently or may potentially work with the program; and the museum director. If there is a voluntary action center in the community, a representative can provide valuable technical assistance as an *ad hoc* committee member or facilitator in planning sessions.

2. Review the museum's mission and long-range plan. Determine how volunteers could help the museum achieve its mission or confirm that the mission of an existing program supports the museum's mission.

3. Conduct a program analysis or self-study. Identify the external factors (for example, economic trends or community demographics) and the internal factors (for example, plans for a major new permanent exhibition gallery or budgetary cutbacks) that affect the volunteer program. Identify the key issues the program will face in the immediate future.

4. Establish (or revise) the mission of the volunteer program. In light of

---

Mission and Goals

FIGURE 2.1

The Cumberland Science Museum

The goals of the volunteer program at the Cumberland Science Museum, Nashville, Tennessee, are closely tied to the mission of the museum.

Museum Mission Statement

The mission of the Cumberland Museum is to provide enjoyable learning experiences in the sciences, technology, history, world cultures, and nature through objects, participatory exhibits, and programs. We do this in order to assist people of all ages in the mastery of concepts and skills necessary to make wise decisions affecting the quality of all life, both now and for future generations.

Volunteer Program Goals

The volunteer program seeks to aid in the accomplishment of the mission of the museum with the following goals:

1. To provide volunteers who will enhance the work of the staff of the museum by complementing, expanding, and supplementing the staff. (No volunteer job is ever designed to take the place of an employee's job.)

2. To work with the museum staff in order to determine the needs for volunteer placement and to design volunteer jobs which will meet the existing, as well as the changing, programs of the museum.

3. To help create and promote in the community an understanding of the museum and all its facets.

4. To meet the community's needs for service, through addressing the individual's needs for serving others, through programs with responsibility and challenge for those qualified, and through career exploration where this will serve the requirements of the museum.

5. To continue to work closely with the Cumberland Museum League, whose purpose it is to support the volunteer movement.

Cumberland Science Museum
800 Ridley Road
Nashville, TN 37203
(615) 259-6099

---

the results of steps two and three, ensure that the mission statement is appropriate to the museum's mission and long-range plan.

5. Set long- and short-range goals and objectives for the volunteer program. Establish broadly stated aims

(goals) for the program, and develop results-oriented statements (objectives) that describe how these aims will be accomplished. Include goals and objectives to be accomplished over a long period as well as those to be achieved in the near term.

FIGURE
2.2

Professional Practices
Sample Guidelines

The Detroit Institute of Arts formally adopted its Guidelines for Professional Practices in 1985. Although designed by and for a particular institution, its basic principles apply to any museum:

Volunteer participation within the Institute is a strong and vital tradition, and the institute programs could not continue without the contributions and personal involvement of devoted volunteers. The staff should be supportive of volunteers, receive them as fellow workers, and willingly provide appropriate training and opportunity for their intellectual enrichment. While volunteers participate in most Institute activities, those with access to the Institute's collections, programs, and associated privileged information work in areas that are sensitive.

Access to the Institute's inner activities is an honor, and the lack of material compensation for effort expended on behalf of the Institute in no way frees the volunteer from adherence to standards that apply to paid staff. The volunteer must work toward the betterment of the institution and not for personal gain other than gratification, knowledge, and enrichment to be derived from museum participation.

Detroit Institute of Arts
5200 Woodward Avenue
Detroit, MI 48202
(313) 833-7900

6. Write policies and procedures. Develop guiding principles and practices—including volunteer job descriptions, recruitment strategies, and a statement of professional standards—for the program's operation. (See Figures 2.2 and 2.3 for examples of professional standards statement.)

7. Submit the plan, along with policies and procedures, to the museum's board of trustees, and, when it is approved, add it to the museum's long-range plan.[1]

Building Organizational Support

A volunteer program must have the commitment and support—both philosophical and practical—of the museum's leadership and paid staff. The board of trustees must enthusiastically subscribe to the ideals and purposes of the volunteer program, and they must demonstrate their commitment through funding and policy guidance. The board and the director must promote a climate of mutual respect by assuring adequate administrative support and space for volunteer activities and by formally recognizing the contributions volunteers and paid staff make together to the museum's public service. The paid staff must understand that volunteers are their partners in the effort to carry out the mission of the museum. The planning process described earlier builds a base of commitment to the program and creates a sense of teamwork among volunteers and staff. The practical aspects of support are then more easily attained.

Volunteer programs are often perceived incorrectly as being free of cost. But just as other museum programs involve overhead as well as direct costs, volunteer programs entail expenses for office space, supplies, printing, mailing, telephone, and other items. The creation of a volunteer program must be accompanied by adequate funding if the program is to survive and thrive. Even a program totally managed by volunteers must have a budget and be accountable for adhering to that budget.

A volunteer program can be fully self-supporting; partially self-supporting with additional support from the museum; or fully supported by the museum budget. Regardless of the source of support, the activities of the program should be subject to the same budgetary approval process as all museum departments and become part of the museum's operating budget. It is not recommended that museum volunteer organizations obtain their own nonprofit status, because this status removes them from the oversight of the museum's administration. Although many volunteer organizations raise their own operating support through activities and dues, they must still obtain the museum director's approval of an annual budget or extraordinary expenditures. The museum director may wish to involve volunteer leaders in the annual budgeting process so that volunteers are a genuine part of financial planning and management.

The volunteer program's expense budget may include such items as office and meeting space; support staff; office expenses (such as postage, mailing, copying, and supplies); office equipment; travel for volunteer organization leaders and the program administrator; training and professional development (including resource materials, speakers' honorariums, and meeting arrangements); recognition activities; and hospitality.

Understanding Legal and Ethical Requirements

A museum's relationship with its volunteer organizations entails potential legal liability for the museum. Many of the volunteer activities that can be so beneficial to a museum—for example, raising funds, selling memberships, or organizing special study tours for members—can also raise liability questions. In addition to complying with federal, state, and local laws, volunteers must also observe standards of ethical behavior that, in the museum profession, sometimes exceed legal requirements.

Legal Liability

To minimize the legal liability of the museum and the volunteer group, a museum must exercise some means of control over its volunteer organizations.

Four areas merit attention: using the museum's name, raising money, using the museum's paid staff to assist the volunteer organization's programs, and undertaking certain types of activities.

The museum's legal counsel should guide the development of an agreement between a museum and a volunteer organization that minimizes legal liability while setting reasonable guidelines for the organization's use of the museum's name, facilities, staff, and collections. The following questions will help determine the areas that should be covered in the agreement:

♦ Does the volunteer organization use the museum's name in fundraising or license commercial use of the name?

♦ Does the organization raise funds on the museum's behalf?

♦ Does the organization hire museum staff members part-time or as consultants, or does it hire its own staff using the museum's Internal Revenue Service employer identification number?

♦ Does the organization hold special events involving liquor service or raffles on the museum premises?

♦ Does the organization sponsor travel programs?

♦ Does the organization sell merchandise based on objects in the museum's collections?

♦ Does the organization hold any off-site events that might require public liability insurance?

♦ Does the organization engage in any income-generating activities that might previously have been tax exempt but may now or in the future be classified as unrelated to the museum's trade or business and therefore be taxable?[2]

Ethical Standards

American museums are organized as public trusts that hold their collections and information for the benefit of those they serve. With this organizational principle come serious responsibilities for museum trustees, staff, and volunteers, who by virtue of their commitment to the museum are committed to serving the interests of the museum's beneficiaries: the public.

Ethical standards for museums have been broadly established for the field by the American Association of Museums and are elaborated on in codes of ethics adopted by individual museums. The *Code of Ethics for Museums* adopted by the AAM in 1991 delineates ethical standards in three areas: governance, collections, and programs. The code states that "loyalty to the mission of the museum and to the public it serves is the essence of museum work, whether volunteer or paid."[3] The Association of Art Museum Directors also has a code of ethics.

Every museum should have a policy on standards of ethical conduct for trustees, staff, and volunteers (Figure 2.3).

Volunteers must understand and clearly abide by these policies, which generally prohibit them from:

♦ receiving compensation (fees, gifts, favors, or other things of value) for duties as a museum volunteer. This restriction also applies to members of the volunteer's immediate household.

♦ violating the confidentiality of privileged information related to museum activities.

♦ using museum property, materials, or supplies for anything other than museum business.

♦ engaging in any outside activity that might result in a conflict of interest—actual, potential, or perceived.

Conflict of interest is an especially critical concern for volunteers. According to the AAMD code, "no individual may use his or her position in a museum for personal gain or to benefit another at the expense of the museum, its mission, its reputation, and the society it serves."[4] When a volunteer's personal or professional loyalties might conflict—or give the appearance of conflicting—with the museum's interests, the potential for conflict of interest exists. A good method of averting the potential for conflict is to ask volunteers to complete a disclosure form that lists areas of personal or professional interest that might pose problems. Simple disclosure may be sufficient, or it may be advisable to assign a volunteer to

Standards for Museum Volunteers

FIGURE 2.3

The volunteer

♦ understands and supports the purpose, structure, and policies of the institution or organization and of the related volunteer group

♦ offers the use of his or her special skills or experience

♦ conducts himself or herself in accordance with the standards of conduct and ethics of the institution or organization

♦ completes any orientation, training course or on-the-job training required

♦ endeavors to be flexible in accepting assignments, performs assigned responsibilities willingly and courteously to the best of his or her ability, and accepts the guidance of his or her manager or supervisors

♦ complies with the time and dress requirements of the institution or organization

♦ obeys all security and safety rules of the institution or organization

♦ respects the confidentiality of sensitive or proprietary information

♦ provides timely notification to his or her supervisor or manager of absence or termination

♦ serves as a goodwill ambassador generally and a communicator of the role of the institution in the community

Source: Endorsed by the American Association for Museum Volunteers Board of Directors, 1991.

FIGURE
2.4

Museum Ethics for Volunteers

The Smithsonian Institution's Guidelines

Ethical standards for Smithsonian Institution volunteers are consistent with standards of conduct for Smithsonian employees and reflect those standards unanimously endorsed by the American Association of Museums for member institutions.

The Smithsonian Institution acknowledges the valuable contribution it receives through the, interest, time, and experience given by volunteers, who serve its various museums and other bureaus and offices. Because of the nature and extent of involvement of volunteers in Smithsonian programs and activities, standards of conduct are set forth for the protection of volunteers and of the Institution.

Volunteer service shall be undertaken for the betterment of the Smithsonian and not for personal gain, other than the inherent reward and personal satisfaction derived from such participation. A Smithsonian volunteer may not accept compensation for performance of Smithsonian tasks as a volunteer. Personal compensation includes gifts, fees, gratuities, or other dispensations to the volunteer or to members of the volunteer's immediate family or household.

Volunteers who have access to museum collections, research, staff activities, and a privileged information must respect the confidentiality of their positions, as well as the significance and integrity of the collections.

To eliminate the possibility of a conflict of interest, each Smithsonian volunteer who is working in an activity area that is related to an outside activity in which the volunteer or a member of his or her family or household is personally involved, or who is active in a related employment or other

---

a job in which the potential for conflict will not arise.

Insurance and Indemnification

Just as the museum often insures board members and professional staff against personal liability, it can provide insurance or indemnification for volunteers. Each state has its own laws governing volunteer liability. To make informed decisions about how much protection exists and how much additional protection is needed, museum adminstrators should consult legal counsel.

Types of insurance that might be in order include:

♦ liability for injury to the volunteer while working on the museum premises, or to others while working for the museum in the community

♦ liability when the volunteer is using his or her own vehicle for museum volunteer work

commercial context, must disclose the nature and extent of such involvement to his/her Smithsonian staff supervisor and whether it is carried out personally or by of the volunteer's immediate family or household. Failure to make a timely disclosure is grounds for dismissal of a volunteer.

Examples of possible conflicts of interest or the appearance of conflicts of interest that require disclosure include:

a. a volunteer working directly with Smithsonian collections if either the volunteer or member of the immediate family or household is involved with collecting or dealing in those same types of objects or materials.

b. a volunteer who serves or contracts to serve as a paid tour guide in a Smithsonian museum.

c. a volunteer holding a paid position or accepting pay for work which is similar or related to the volunteer's duties at the Smithsonian.

In many situations it will be sufficient for the volunteer to disclose the outside activity that might be a conflict of interest. In certain cases, the volunteer may be asked to serve in other Smithsonian activities where there is not an actual or apparent conflict of interest. In an extreme case, the volunteer may be asked to terminate Smithsonian service so that his or her other activities might be pursued without any conflict of interest.

Smithsonian staff supervisors must make a written record of disclosures by volunteers assigned to them and if there might appear to be a conflict of interest, consult with a Smithsonian Ethics Counselor in the Office of General Counsel.

These standards represent basic principles for ethical conduct by Smithsonian volunteers. The directors of Smithsonian bureaus and offices may adopt more detailed guidelines if consistent with the principles outlined in this office memorandum (OM 827).

Source: Visitor Information and
Associates' Reception Center
Smithsonian Institution
Washington, DC 20560

♦ bonding for museum volunteers who handle money (for example, museum store volunteers or committee treasurers)

♦ liability of the museum for fund-raising practices of the volunteer organization

♦ liability if a third party is injured because of the actions of volunteers or in cases of discrimination by volunteers toward other volunteers

Establishing a Program Structure

Once the program has formulated its mission, goals, and objectives and developed a base of support from the museum's leadership, the next step is to establish an operating structure. In an existing volunteer program, a periodic assessment of the operating structure is a useful planning and management tool. The program may have grown so large that it needs to be streamlined to restore efficiency, or the structure may be too complicated and require simplification to renew the enthusiasm of volunteers weighed down with paperwork and reporting systems. Whether creating a new program or reorganizing an existing one, an important point to remember is the value of involving experienced volunteers as active participants in management.

When thinking about a volunteer program's operating structure, it is useful to first consider the program's stage of organizational development. Organizations generally progress through three stages: emerging, evolving, and mature. For volunteer programs, these stages are present in every type of museum and under many different circumstances.

Emerging Programs

Emerging volunteer programs may be closely allied with the goals of the program's founder or founders. The founder might be someone from the community or a member of the museum's board. In either case, the founder is apt to be a charismatic individual with the vision to create a new program. Many years after such programs are launched, volunteers may remember how exciting it was to be part of the first activities. A new volunteer program can be founded to serve an express purpose—to sponsor a special event, help with a special exhibition, or begin weekend interpretive programs. Or an emerging program can exist in a museum that is founded and staffed entirely by volunteers. New programs

sometimes do not begin with the planning process described earlier in this chapter.

The structure of an emerging program often involves a group of volunteers reporting to a single leader. As long as the operation remains small, the leader is able to keep track of the day-to-day work of the volunteers. As the volume of work increases, more volunteers are added. Efficiency may begin to falter if the leader continues to take responsibility for all major decisions rather than training others and delegating authority for day-to-day decisions and for managing major projects. In all-volunteer museums where the personnel are mostly part-time individuals who have other demands on their time, a smoothly managed organization is especially important.

Evolving Programs

In the evolving volunteer program, the organization has advanced by two or three generations from its origins. There are more volunteers, some of whom have never known the founder. There are also more volunteer projects in addition to the project that the original group was created to carry out. A hierarchy of leaders who make decisions and manage the program has begun to develop. The evolving program usually has no mission statement or long-range plan, but its leaders are ready for change and know they need to solidify the program's foundation to provide direction for the future.

Evolving programs frequently exist in all-volunteer museums that are ready to begin the transition to forming a paid staff. In such a museum, the transition from one organizational stage to the next may be trying. If paid staff are hired, the volunteer working in a staff-like role may have to give up hands-on, operational work. Volunteers who ran all aspects of the museum before the paid staff arrived must be able to limit their roles to being volunteers under the supervision of the new staff members. The transition is eased by open communication and a clear understanding of the museum's organizational structure.

Mature Programs

The mature program evolves naturally from the emerging program. If the program has grown and volunteers have been trained to assume greater responsibility, the all-volunteer program can make a smooth transition to a departmentalized program within the museum. A long-range planning process is critical at this stage.

In the mature program, the chief volunteer leader is supported by volunteer committee chairpersons. Decisions that were once the exclusive purview of the leader are now delegated to the chairpersons. A reporting system allows this group of volunteer leaders to carry on operations without the chief volunteer's approval or oversight. Procedures and policies are established and volunteer jobs are defined. This structure enables a small staff to work with a large volunteer force. It depends upon identifying volunteer leaders to serve in middle management positions.

A volunteer program in the mature stage sets goals that are aligned with the museum's mission and part of the museum's long-range planning. The policies and procedures for volunteer projects and programs provide a structure while stimulating creativity and enthusiasm. The leaders of large volunteer programs must remember to allow individual volunteers the flexibility to develop new programs within the system. All volunteers appreciate the freedom to achieve and to receive personal satisfaction.

Two Volunteer Program Structures

Museum volunteer programs can be organized according to one of two models: an *independent supporting organization* or an *integrated volunteer program* with paid or unpaid staff administrator. These models do not always operate discretely; one or both of them may exist simultaneously. Some institutions have both models operating among various volunteer groups, providing a wide range of options for volunteer service. Any program—whether managed by volunteers or by an administrator—can be highly professional as long as there is good communication, mutual respect, and commitment to the museum's goals.

The following questions can guide the choice of model or models for a particular institution:

1. What is the program's stage of organizational development?

2. How have volunteer services traditionally been structured in the museum?

3. What proportion of volunteer activities is devoted to:
   public programs?
   visitor services?
   behind-the-scenes activities?
   fund raising and special events?
   community relations?

4. What staff resources are available to administer and support the volunteer program?

Independent Supporting Organization

The independent supporting organization's policies and procedures are not part of the parent museum's operations, and volunteers are members of a separate entity (see Figure 2.5). The organization may have its own bylaws, governance structure, and tax-exempt status apart from those of the museum. To promote accountability and open communication, a supporting organization should have a formal agreement with the museum.

Depending on the type of museum and its mission, such an organization may provide a variety of the volunteer services described in chapter 1. New types of supporting organizations are frequently created in museums to meet any one or a number of broad purposes, including fund raising and special events; support of interpretive programs or administration of the complete interpretive function; and providing behind-the-scenes assistance.

Effective supporting organizations are usually highly structured with detailed rules and regulations governing volunteer responsibilities, conduct, minimum service requirements, and ethics. Such organizations provide extensive training, including in-service management programs for experienced volunteers and special lectures to increase the volunteers' knowledge of their vital role in the work of the museum. Many such organizations give volunteers provisional membership status for a specified period, after which the individual's work is evaluated and he or she is considered for full membership.

Supporting organizations typically work in partnership with paid staff. Each of the organization's programmatic and administrative functions is usually under the aegis of a committee that includes a staff liaison. This paid staff member, the museum director, and sometimes the board of trustees are involved in the approval process for volunteer programs.

Integrated Program with Administrator

Some volunteer programs, after operating successfully for years with volunteers totally in charge, find that they need an administrator when the program becomes too large to manage with part-

FIGURE
2.5

Independent Supporting Organization

Wadsworth Atheneum

The Women's Committee of the Wadsworth Atheneum (WCWA), in Hartford, Connecticut, is a broad-reaching, active, exciting, and visible group within the museum structure. Founded 40 years ago, the WCWA continues to expand its involvement without overstepping and endangering its museum relationship and with its own evaluation and advisory systems in place. The WCWA "belongs" to its members and is not directed by the museum through a volunteer administrator. The committee can effect change, growth, and direction of its own organization, but it is constantly aware that its mission is to serve the museum's needs.

This symbiotic relationship between volunteer and museum is maintained through well-planned lines of communication. The WCWA president meets regularly with the museum director and sits on the board of trustees. The museum services manager reviews and assists with the use of museum facilities for all events and is the staff member most directly involved with the committee. The public relations coordinator approves and offers assistance for all press releases, advertisements, invitations, and other similar material written by the WCWA. The membership director provides mailing lists, which are often updated by volunteers. The museum shop manager and the information desk coordinator provide on-site orientation for new volunteers.

The WCWA is led by an Executive Committee with twelve members, seven of whom are officers elected annually. The rest are appointed by the WCWA president. Under the aegis of the Finance Committee, the WCWA has its own checking accounts and is responsible for all financial transactions resulting from WCWA activities. Quarterly reports are presented to the museum controller and the WCWA board and membership. At year's end all WCWA accounts are audited by the museum's auditor. All monies raised by the WCWA, except the portion needed to fund committee activities, are turned over to the museum. The committee chooses how these funds are to be used: examples include renovating a gallery, funding a major exhibit, and purchasing office computers.

Given the decreasing pool of volunteers, a self-directed, self-managed independent supporting organization can be an extremely satisfying opportunity.

Excerpted from Elizabeth N. Muench, "Volunteer Programs Run by Volunteers," *AAMV*, Spring 1990, p. 2.

time volunteer leadership. The administrator may be paid or unpaid. (For a discussion of the responsibilities and qualifications of a volunteer program administrator, see chapter 3.) In this model (Figure 2.6), which is appropriate for institutions of all sizes, the volunteer program is a separate function within a

FIGURE
2.6

Integrated Volunteer Program

Maine Maritime Museum

Located in the historic shipbuilding town of Bath, Maine, the Maine Maritime Museum attracts dedicated volunteers who are committed to the museum's mission of keeping seafaring traditions alive. Volunteers work alongside the twenty paid staff members throughout the museum, doing everything from helping with yard work to handling and taking inventory of the collections to conducting interpretive programs. There are about 100 active volunteers.

The Maine Maritime Museum's volunteer program is fully administered by a paid coordinator on the staff of the Department of Public Programs. Her role is similar to that of a personnel manager and encompasses job design, recruitment and selection, training, scheduling, and evaluation. She has a dual role as educational programs coordinator. There is no committee or organization of volunteers; the coordinator is their link with the museum. She holds monthly meetings for volunteers with guest speakers on topics related to the museum's collections and programs and publishes a newsletter to keep volunteers informed. Museum departments let her know about their needs for volunteer assistance, and she develops jobs and selects the appropriate people to fill them. Training takes place twice a year and involves both paid staff members and outside experts. Staff are also encouraged to attend meetings of volunteers, and there is close interaction among paid and unpaid staff.

As the demand for volunteers increases at the Maine Maritime Museum, the administrative structure is responding. The volunteer coordinator supervises only those volunteers assigned to public and educational programs; other paid staff share supervisory duties. More intensive and more frequent volunteer training is planned.

Without volunteers, says coordinator Carole Farnham, "we certainly could not function as well. . . . Thank heavens we have a very dedicated group!"

Maine Maritime Museum
243 Washington Street
Bath, ME 04530
(207) 443-1316

department or a separate department equal in stature to other museum departments.

This model works differently depending on the museum. In some museums the volunteer program administrator directs visitor service and certain behind-the-scenes activities, while the education department supervises volunteers who undertake interpretive activities and the development department has responsibility for volunteers who raise funds. In other museums the volunteer program administrator supervises all volunteers regardless of the type of work they do. Whatever the reporting system, the integrated volunteer program with an administrator is part of the museum's administrative structure; the professional practices and personnel policies applicable to volunteers are similar to those for paid staff.

In this model, program planning committees are joint volunteer/paid staff task forces. Paid staff and volunteers both participate in the administration of day-to-day activities. For this model to be effective, there must be open communication, with volunteers having a voice in planning the museum programs that involve their services.

Armed with a long-range plan, carefully thought-out policies and procedures, the support of the museum's board and administration, and an appropriate operating structure, volunteer leaders can begin to work out the details of day-to-day program administration.

3

OPTIONS FOR LEADERSHIP

VOLUNTEER
PROGRAM
ADMINISTRATION

The extensive services volunteers provide to museums and museum visitors are supported behind the scenes by an operational structure that keeps the volunteer program running smoothly and functioning for the benefit of the institution and its public. In many museums—small and large—a paid or unpaid administrator is responsible for day-to-day program operations. In other museums, volunteer leaders handle administrative tasks, sometimes using a system of "day captains." Effective supervision of volunteers, carefully crafted job descriptions, and a well-organized record-keeping system are all essential to sound administration.

The Volunteer Administrator's Role

Deciding whether to appoint an administrator is a key step in a volunteer program's organizational development. Programs that have reached the mature stage (see chapter 2) are ready to achieve departmental status in the museum. They usually have a complex reporting structure, many volunteers, and multiple projects and activities. Program administration has become a multifaceted and time-consuming task that can no longer be carried out solely by board members and committee chairs. The volunteer program needs the focused support and administrative continuity that a full- or part-time staff administrator can provide.

The volunteer program administrator—whether paid or unpaid, full-time or part-time—is a highly important component of a volunteer organization. The administrator's office maintains continuity, direction, and momentum in the program, serves as the center for volunteer administrative tasks, and is the catalyst for assessment and planning. The administrator's role in the organizational structure of the institution must be endorsed by both the administration and the volunteers. He or she must have sufficient stature, knowledge, and experience to work effectively with volunteer leadership and advise the administration in matters related to the volunteer program.

The primary benefits of appointing a volunteer administrator are continuity and efficiency. An administrator can streamline the recruitment, selection, and training of volunteers; consolidate a variety of volunteer activities under a central office; coordinate the development and implementation of performance standards for volunteers; and increase the visibility of the program.

The size of the museum, availability of resources, and program size are among the factors that determine whether the administrator is paid or unpaid. In many programs, an elected or appointed volunteer leader will undertake for one or two years responsibilities similar to those of a paid volunteer administrator. This arrangement can be successful if the candidate chosen has the appropriate experience and qualifications for the job, is committed to devoting full time (or the necessary part-time hours) to the complex task of program administration, and will provide continuity by serving as administrator for a sufficient period.

Responsibilities and Qualifications of the Volunteer Administrator

The job of the volunteer program administrator varies from museum to museum, but generally it entails the following responsibilities. The administrator

FIGURE
3.1

Sample Job Description

Volunteer Administrator

The volunteer administrator is responsible for the development, organization, operation, supervision, evaluation, and maintenance of museum volunteer activities. In so doing the administrator works with museum staff at all levels, observes established museum policies and procedures, promotes the professional use of volunteers, and utilizes recruitment methods to assure a balance of age, gender, and ethnicity within the volunteer corps. The administrator

♦ develops volunteer programs and services responsive to the needs of the museum

♦ defines the parameters, organization, and responsibilities of the volunteer programs and/or services

♦ establishes and/or facilitates training appropriate to the programs and/or services to be provided by volunteers

♦ recruits, screens, and selects volunteers utilizing methods that assure appropriate program placement and a balance of age, gender, and ethnicity within the volunteer corps

♦ supervises volunteer activities, reviews individual performance and provides supplemental training and counseling as needed

♦ evaluates volunteer programs and services, determining their viability

♦ maintains volunteer programs and services by providing appropriate administrative support, volunteer recognition and appreciation activities, and benefits commensurate with museum unpaid employee status

♦ formulates an annual budget, maintaining administrative oversight, and carries out assigned personnel functions in accordance with individual museum policies and procedures

♦ serves as a communication link between administration and volunteers

♦ represents the museum and its volunteer programs to the community at large

♦ understands, supports, and promotes the complementary missions of the museum and the volunteer program

♦ acts as liaison between the volunteer program and museum staff

♦ coordinates recruitment, placement, and training of volunteers

♦ establishes evaluation criteria for individual volunteers

♦ maintains up-to-date records on volunteers and the volunteer program

♦ initiates periodic assessments of the volunteer program

♦ represents the volunteer program in the community

♦ seeks continuing professional development opportunities

To carry out these responsibilities effectively, the person selected as volunteer administrator must be a committed leader and advocate, a capable manager, and a good communicator.

Leadership and Advocacy

First and foremost, the volunteer manager must be personally dedicated to the importance of volunteering in museums and work internally to promote this dedication among staff at all levels and among volunteers. He or she must also understand the motivations people have for volunteering in a museum; this quality helps the administrator provide leadership for volunteers while assuring that the mission of the volunteer organization supports the mission of the institution. Some administrators have arrived at their positions through volunteering for the museum. Equipped with this experience, they are sometimes better suited to the position than others who have no background as museum volunteers.

Management

The volunteer administrator must be skilled at administering a complex program that serves all areas of the institution and involves volunteers and paid staff in diverse activities. The ability to work through others to achieve goals is an essential quality, whether those "others" are a 400-member volunteer council or a paid staff who must be convinced that volunteers are an asset. The administrator must have the creativity and the flexibility to identify opportunities for volunteer work in the museum and involve others in translating these opportunities into reality. Motivational and supervisory skills are also critical. The administrator must actively promote the principle of teamwork, urging volunteers and staff to join in working toward a common mission. He or she must also hold volunteers accountable for their role on the staff by promoting high standards in volunteer performance.

Communication

The administrator of volunteers must communicate effectively with a variety of groups and individuals both inside and outside the institution. He or she is the critical link between staff and volunteers, promoting open dialogue, cooperative problem-solving, and, most important, teamwork on behalf of the museum. The administrator knows which staff members are most effective at working with volunteers and are willing to invest the necessary training and supervision time to help the program be a success.

As a representative of the volunteer program, the administrator should also be visible in the community. Broad-based community involvement through contacts with other organizations will attract new volunteers to the museum. The volunteer administrator can be even more effective if he or she joins and participates actively in several community groups.

Reporting Structure for the Volunteer Administrator

The volunteer program administrator may report to any of several departments, including:

♦ the director, if the program is small or if it serves all of the programs of the institution equally

♦ the independent supporting organization, if the administrator has been hired to support its activities only

♦ the education director, if the program is focused primarily on public programs

♦ the education director or public affairs director, if the program handles visitor services

♦ the museum's administrator, if the program's primary purpose is to provide routine staff support

♦ the director of development or membership, if the program is focused on fund raising.

The administrator of the volunteer program will be most effective if he or she reports to the director or other senior staff. A program that has no direct line of communication to the top can have little impact on general planning and may be viewed as peripheral and unessential to the rest of museum's functions.

Transition to Paid or Unpaid Administration

When the position of volunteer program administrator is created, volunteers should be prepared for changes and encouraged to support the new administrator. Volunteer leaders may participate in the development of a volunteer administrator's job description and possibly in the interview process to ensure support of the new position. A further way to smooth the transition is for the volunteer group to appoint a committee to advise and consult with the administrator. There are mutual benefits to this collaborative approach. The administrator learns from the volunteers' experience, while the volunteers profit from the administrator's fresh perspective. Together they can evaluate the need for change and avoid hasty decisions that might disrupt continuity. The new administrator should remember to give full credit and praise to those who have developed the program.

Professional Development for the Volunteer Administrator

The volunteer administrator will benefit greatly from participation in professional activities such as training workshops and seminars, conferences, and formal or informal networks of colleagues. The museum also benefits by supporting the administrator's involvement in these activities. When funding is needed to take advantage of professional development opportunities, the museum should consider providing it.

Ample opportunities exist for the administrator to be involved in the museum and volunteer administration professions. Meetings of national, regional, state, and local organizations give the administrator a chance to meet colleagues in other cultural institutions and keep up to date on current issues and professional practices. Some of these organizations sponsor training workshops and seminars. Local "roundtable" groups of administrators from cultural institutions in the museum's area are good forums for initiating collaboration among institutions, getting to know colleagues, and sharing ideas. The oldest such group is New York City's Volunteer Program Administrators in Cultural Institutions, whose 130 members meet monthly for discussions of issues of common concern (see the Resource Guide for names of similar organizations).

In the volunteer administration field, the Association for Volunteer Administration (AVA) not only provides a wide variety of services to professional volunteer administrators but offers a performance-based certification program for volunteer administrators. The National VOLUNTEER Center sponsors meetings and publishes books and pamphlets on volunteer issues. Chapters of the American Society of Directors of Volunteer Services and state and local offices of vol-

unteerism can be found in every state. Involvement in local branches of such organizations can expand the administrator's professional network; it can also help dispel the aura of elitism that sometimes surrounds cultural institutions and enhance the reputation of the museum as a community service institution.

A profession becomes truly legitimate when its members are trained at professional institutes and at institutions of higher education. In 1992, the Association for Volunteer Administration compiled a comprehensive list of volunteer management education programs in the United States and Canada and found that course offerings ranged from one-day workshops to graduate degree programs. The curriculums generally focused on management, program administration, and communications skills. Museums that hire an administrator from the ranks of their volunteers might consider supporting the administrator's training in one of these programs to enhance management skills, earn a degree, or become certified in volunteer management. An administrator who has achieved the status of certified volunteer administrator through the Association for Volunteer Administration will earn respect for the volunteer program in the professional community, the local community, and the museum itself.

Volunteer Supervision

A successful volunteer program has individuals on the museum staff who believe in the value of volunteer contributions to the museum and are willing to devote time to nurturing committed volunteers to help fulfill the museum's mission and achieve departmental goals. Although sometimes volunteers themselves will be in supervisory positions, it is more common that paid staff members will be directly responsible for on-the-job training and ongoing supervision of volunteers working on department assignment. Sometimes the volunteer administrator has responsibility for volunteer supervision throughout the institution, but especially in larger museums, the job is delegated to other paid staff. Supervisors should be available to volunteers on a daily basis. The positions need not necessarily be held by management staff.

Guidelines for Paid Staff Supervisors

Staff supervisors of volunteers have a variety of functions (see Figure 3.2). In museums that have an administrator, a number of these duties are a team effort between the administrator and the supervisor. The following guidelines will help volunteer administrators and staff supervisors promote a productive relationship with volunteers.

1. *Inform the volunteer administrator in a timely fashion about the needs for volunteers.* The more demanding the job, the more time it takes to recruit the right volunteer.

2. *Plan volunteer training thoroughly.* Before the volunteer begins the job, the administrator and supervisor should develop a job description and training plan for the position. They should make every effort to avoid a situation in which a supervisor gives cursory or unclear directions, is too busy to answer questions, or is vague about his or her expectations for the volunteer. (See chapter 5 for more information about training.)

3. *Establish a positive recognition system.* The staff supervisor should meet regularly to keep the volunteer administrator informed about volunteers' performance. Supervisors should never fail to let the administrator know about volunteers who deserve special recognition for superior work or consistent dedication. (See chapter 5 for further discussion of volunteer recognition.)

4. *Explain departmental policies and procedures clearly.* When volunteers understand how a particular department works and how their own position fits in, they will feel part of a team that is making a significant contribution to the museum. Staff supervisors should emphasize procedures for recordkeeping, scheduling, and departure from the position; they should also remember to keep volunteers abreast of new developments or changes in policies and procedures.

5. *Know how to deal with an unproductive or dissatisfied volunteer.* When supervisors suffer from the misconception that volunteers can-

FIGURE 3.2

Staff Supervisor Responsibilities

The staff supervisor of volunteers

♦ attends supervisory training

♦ works with the volunteer administrator or appropriate volunteer organization committee to clearly define the volunteer positions that the supervisor is requesting

♦ participates with the volunteer administrator in the selection of volunteers for the position

♦ provides specific on-site training for volunteers

♦ provides comfortable work space and is ready with materials and instructions for volunteers when they report to work

♦ has regular contact with volunteers and conducts an annual formal evaluation

♦ communicates key information to volunteers that will affect their performance (such as schedule changes, meeting dates, and current program and exhibition information)

♦ maintains good records of volunteer service, including hours and tasks completed

♦ participates in planning and implementation of formal and informal volunteer recognition activities

♦ notifies the volunteer administrator or volunteer committee chair of any problems or questions regarding a volunteer as soon as they become evident

♦ advises the volunteer administrator or volunteer committee chair when a volunteer terminates and/or has a change in status

♦ encourages other staff to participate in volunteer orientation and training appropriate to their discipline so that they can establish rapport with volunteers

♦ expects that volunteers will respect the demands of the supervisor's job responsibilities

♦ views volunteers as unpaid professional staff and provides them the respect that staff members receive

Sources:
Philadelphia Museum of Art
Detroit Institute of Arts
Catholic Charities of the Archdiocese of St. Paul and Minneapolis

not be dismissed, the morale and work of paid staff and other volunteers—as well as the experience of museum visitors—can be affected. Supervisors must also be responsive to dissatisfied volunteers, who may simply be seeking to improve communication, resolve problems, or clarify questions.

Training and Support for Paid Staff Supervisors

Whether the choice is formal training or informal guidance, department administrators must support the training and development of paid staff who supervise volunteers. Training and professional growth opportunities should not be viewed as unwelcome, unscheduled interruptions in the work day but as efforts that benefit the department and the entire institution.

A volunteer management handbook is a useful guide for all who supervise volunteers. The handbook can be introduced during the supervisors' training and kept in each museum department. The information can also be incorporated into the museum's personnel handbook. The handbook should include:

♦ annual calendar of volunteer activities, training sessions, tours, required meetings, and special events

♦ requirements and procedures for supervisors

♦ requirements and procedures for volunteers

♦ current volunteer job descriptions

♦ volunteer request form and description of procedures

♦ sample service record form or time sheet and evaluation forms

♦ statement of professional standards and ethics for volunteers

Designing Volunteer Jobs

A volunteer program with diverse job opportunities will attract the interest of people of all ages, interests, and backgrounds. The volunteer administrator, paid staff, and volunteers themselves should always be alert to new possibilities for volunteer assistance.

The idea for a volunteer job may originate with museum staff who need assistance in their daily responsibilities, or volunteers may propose the creation of particular jobs that they feel would contribute something to the museum. The need for a volunteer job may also emerge in planning a special project. For all-volunteer projects such as special events or fund-raising activities, the need for volunteer jobs is self-evident. Or it may be clear that to attract working people as volunteers, jobs must be created that have evening and weekend schedules.

No matter how the idea originates, every volunteer task should have a clearly stated purpose. When designing new volunteer jobs or evaluating the effectiveness of existing positions, the following questions from a handbook for British volunteer administrators serve as guidelines:

♦ Is the job needed?

♦ How does it contribute to the museum's goals and volunteer policy?

♦ Why should a volunteer do it? A voluntary post should not replace a paid post. The aim is to supplement, not supplant, paid staff.

♦ Do the specific duties allocated to each job allow the volunteer room for individual development and a career path?

♦ Does the job fit the time frame of the volunteer?

♦ Are the specific policies and procedures involved understood by staff and volunteers?

♦ Does [the job] constitute humane, interesting work, providing satisfaction, a sense of belonging, and a chance to learn?[1]

Positive responses to these questions indicate that the volunteer job will have a solid foundation within the museum and be central to the museum's purposes. If an existing job no longer meets these criteria, it should be redesigned or eliminated. Unrealistic or poorly conceived jobs that are not really needed in the museum will not sustain volunteer commitment and can damage the volunteer program's effectiveness.

Writing Job Descriptions

Every volunteer job should have a clear written description that includes the following information:

♦ Objectives: Why is the job needed? What audience will be served? How does the job enhance the museum's mission? What is the volunteer expected to accomplish?

♦ Responsibilities: What specific tasks will the volunteer do to carry out the objectives of the job? How does the volunteer job relate to staff responsibilities?

♦ Qualifications: What skills, work experience (including volunteer), education, or knowledge are required?

♦ Time commitment: How much time per week or per day will the volunteer be expected to contribute? What are the specific hours of the job, if any? Is the assignment short-term or long-term? What is the policy regarding departure?

♦ Reporting structure: To whom will the volunteer report?

♦ Training: What training will the museum provide for the job?

♦ Evaluation: What form will job evaluation take and how frequently will it occur?

Responsibility for preparing the job description depends on the individual museum. Often paid staff members write job descriptions for each position for which they need volunteers, and the volunteer administrator then reviews the descriptions. Sometimes the volunteer administrator writes the job descriptions, or the responsibility falls to the volunteer chairperson of a particular project or event. The job description should be prepared with the same care that is exercised in writing a job description for a paid staff member.

Many volunteers find jobs in which they can make decisions more appealing than jobs in which they cannot. Others are looking for opportunities to use or improve their word-processing or other office skills. Even jobs like stuffing enve-

FIGURE 3.3

Volunteer Job Descriptions

Lincoln Park Zoo, Chicago

Position: Docent

Supervisor:

Children's Zoo—Children's Zoo Curator and Assigned Animal Keepers

Education Department—Curator of Education and Assigned Zoo Instructors

Volunteer Department—Director of Volunteer Services and Assigned Senior Docent

Objective:

To promote positive awareness of wildlife to the general public and to communicate established educational concepts which underlie zoo programs, Children's Zoo exhibits and program design.

Responsibilities:

Conduct tours, exhibit talks, animal presentations and observations. Transport animals to Chicago teaching locations. Implement established education programs at the Children's Zoo, including animal handling, animal talks, informal sharing of information with visitors, facilitating education activities and systems in Kids' Corner. Assist instructors with classes.

Qualifications:

An interest in wildlife, conservation and teaching. Must be enthusiastic, flexible and responsible. Ability to work well as a team member is important. Assignment requires handling small animals (guinea pig, rabbit, ferret, hedgehog, armadillo, pygmy goat), birds and non-poisonous snakes and speaking to groups of children and adults, indoors and out.

Training:

Zoo staff provides general orientation and specific training in zoology and wildlife conservation, animal handling, Kids' Corner, animal exhibit talks and other hands-on activities.

Requirements:

Attend training, pass oral examinations and make a regular weekly commitment of a minimum of four hours per week for two years. A valid tetanus shot is required.

Lincoln Park Zoological Society
2200 North Cannon Drive
Chicago, IL 60604
(312) 935-6700

lopes can be rewarding when done by groups of volunteers who know they are making a much-appreciated contribution to the museum and can share social time as they work in a group. If the importance of a volunteer job can be explained in the context of the overall mission of the department and the museum, the value of routine jobs will be recognized.

Volunteer Job Descriptions

Utah State Historical Society

Position: Bookstore salesclerk

Supervisor:

Bookstore Manager supervises and coordinates the volunteers in the bookstore.

Location:

The Society is housed at the former Denver & Rio Grande Railroad depot, one of Utah's great historical buildings.

Duties:

Greet the public, provide them with information about bookstore items and assist them in purchasing merchandise.

Receive incoming calls, provide information, record messages and refer patrons to appropriate division offices.

Rings up merchandise sales on cash register and credit card machine.

Package and mail catalog and bookstore orders.

Stocking shelves, light dusting, arranging displays.

Skills:

Familiarity with computerized cash register system or willingness to learn.

Telephone skills, basic math, legible handwriting.

Courteous, helpful, willing to work with the public.

Able to handle occasional pressure and hectic situations.

Interest in Utah and western history.

Importance of volunteer positions to the Society:

The bookstore is an extension of the educational program of the Historical Society. Its operation is of great importance as a source of revenue for the Historical Society. The bookstore carries with it important obligations to the public to ensure quality and authenticity.

Benefits:

The satisfaction of valuable service rendered to the Utah State Historical Society, the schools, the community and to visitors from all parts of the world.

Training and work experience to maintain old skills and develop new ones.

Along with regular staff, active volunteers will receive a 15% discount on all USHS gift and bookstore purchases.

Invitations to occasional tours to other museums, historic sites and private collections.

A written record of volunteer service for related work or school purposes.

Commitment:

Bookstore volunteers must be able to make a commitment for a one-year period. Volunteers must be able to work a minimum of one four-hour shift per week unless prior arrangements have been made.

Training:

On-site training in bookstore policy and procedures.

Working Conditions:

Normal office working conditions, some light lifting required.

Utah State Historical Society
300 Rio Grande
Salt Lake City, UT 84101
(801) 533-5755

Volunteer Job Descriptions

Seattle Art Museum

Museum Departments

Assist museum staff departments such as Volunteer, Education, Curatorial, Development, Registrar, and Public Relations. Available weekly during regular museum office hours. Position usually requires a six-month minimum commitment, typing and computer skills, attention to detail. Limited opportunities for college interns.

Hospitality/Special Events

Serve as a host or hostess at members' previews and other special events. Work approximately one evening per month. Warm, professional public presence; knowledge of museum programs helpful. Ability to stand for extended periods of time.

Basic Requirements for Seattle Art Museum (SAM) Volunteers

1. All volunteers are required to be SAM members. Members receive regular program information important for all volunteers. Contact the volunteer coordinator if this is a problem for you.

2. Most volunteer positions require a one-year minimum commitment.

3. Volunteers are responsible for attending the orientation and training sessions related to their volunteer committee or department.

4. Volunteers are required to attend regular docent or staff tours of the current special exhibition and/or permanent collections.

5. We encourage volunteers to attend museum previews and events.

Seattle Art Museum
Seattle WA
(206) 625-8900

Maintaining Records and Reports

Accurate record keeping provides valuable statistics for the museum's use as well as necessary information for program evaluation. Calculating and reporting the value of volunteer services, for example, can help a museum enhance its budget justifications and funding proposals. Maintaining complete program histories and service records enables a volunteer program to assess how well it is serving the museum's needs and simplify program planning.

Record-keeping tools include individual volunteer work reports, in which each volunteer records hours served and other details of the assignment. Narrative

FIGURE 3.4 Assessing Staff Year Savings of a Volunteer Program

The Smithsonian Institution uses this formula to assess the value of volunteer contributions in time and expertise:

1. Add up the number of hours contributed by all volunteers during the year.

2. Divide this number by the number of actual hours per year worked by a full-time employee, excluding lunch hours and sick and annual leave. The result gives the number of full-time staff years worked by volunteers.

Source: Visitor Information and
Associates Reception Center
Smithsonian Institution
Washington, DC 20560
(202) 357-2700

project reports, which are prepared by the volunteer administrator, staff supervisor, or volunteer leader in charge, summarize the project, give a financial report, and make recommendations for improvement. Individual volunteer records are also important when museum volunteer experience is used in a resumé.

Choices about a volunteer program's administration are guided by the organizational structure and requirements of the museum, the nature of the program, and the needs of the visitors the museum serves. More important than the details of program administration—which vary from museum to museum—is the creation of a suitable structure and the commitment to professional practices. From this foundation the program will be able to recruit people from all parts of the community who are eager to join in the rewarding and exciting work of volunteering for the museum.

CULTIVATING VOLUNTEER INTEREST

RECRUITMENT AND
SELECTION

Volunteer leaders agree that the volunteer force is changing everywhere, and museums are no exception. The "traditional" volunteers—married women who are not employed—have been joined by men and women of all ages and socioeconomic and ethnic backgrounds, from retired people to high school students to business executives. Economic and social trends continue to affect the volunteer pool from which museums recruit. According to recent information from the Gallup Organization, two-thirds of today's volunteers are working people.[1]

Understanding these shifts in the characteristics, motivation, and availability of volunteers is critical to the success of any recruitment effort (see Figure 4.1). More and more museum volunteer administrators are working to match opportunities with available volunteers and

FIGURE 4.1

The Changing Faces of Volunteers

Marlene Wilson, an expert in volunteer administration, describes some characteristics of this expanded volunteer pool. It includes

♦ baby boomers, who are well educated, highly skilled, often working professionals, and sometimes single parents. People in this age group (born between 1945 and 1964) make up 45 percent of the adult population and are willing to volunteer when volunteer jobs are tailored to the realities of their lives.

♦ the "sandwich" generation (born between 1925 and 1945), who are facing the reality of caring for aging family members as well as returning children.

This group has been the mainstay of many volunteer programs but is now beginning to say "no."

♦ senior citizens, the most rapidly growing group. Studies have shown that active, regular volunteering is an important factor in keeping healthy.

♦ minority populations, who are underrepresented in museum volunteer ranks. In the 1990 census, one in four Americans defined themselves as people of color.

Source: "Marlene Wilson Challenges Museum Volunteer Managers," *AAMV*, Winter 1992, p. 11.

create new types of positions that capitalize on the versatility of individuals in the volunteer pool. They are recruiting from new sources, not only because fewer volunteers are available through traditional sources but because they want to welcome a broader spectrum of the public into the museum and involve them as volunteers. They are marketing the volunteer program to the community in imaginative ways, keeping in mind both the needs of the museum and the interests and abilities of potential volunteers.

The recruitment and selection process has four parts: developing recruitment goals, identifying sources of volunteers in the community and planning appropriate recruitment methods, interviewing prospective volunteers and

evaluating candidates and making selections.

Developing Recruitment Goals

Volunteer recruitment and selection are usually the responsibility of the volunteer program administrator with the participation of a committee of volunteers. If there is no administrator, the committee usually recruits and selects volunteers. Sometimes an advisory group of community leaders is helpful in attracting a broad-based group of volunteers; the use of advisory groups is discussed later in this chapter.

An essential preliminary step in the recruitment process is the design and description of volunteer jobs that both meet the needs of the museum's various departments and provide productive, rewarding work for volunteers (see chapter 3). Up-to-date, realistic job descriptions are the foundation for the recruitment process. Other factors, including the program's structure and procedures, the availability of volunteers in the community, and the museum's interest in targeting specific populations as volunteers, should also be taken into account. The following checklist will help shape the recruitment process:

1. *Schedule.* Is there a schedule for recruitment, or does the program recruit year-round? In the latter case, staff need to continually orient and train new volunteers. Is this feasible?

2. *Time.* When are volunteers needed the most? Are they available when needed? Should meeting and training times be changed to attract available volunteers?

3. *Location.* Is the museum served by adequate public transportation systems? Is there safe free or inexpensive parking for volunteers?

4. *Recruitment agencies.* Has the program contacted the local voluntary action center? Does the administrator or a volunteer leader attend meetings of professional volunteer administrators?

5. *Organizations.* Are there community organizations with interests similar to those of the museum? Are there clubs and special groups that have an interest in subjects covered by the museum's collection? Are there historical societies, artists' groups, retired teachers' organizations, mineral and gem societies, or other organizations whose members might like to become involved as volunteers?

6. *Membership.* Has an appeal been issued to the museum's membership for new volunteers? Does the museum regularly feature volunteer needs and activities in its membership mailings and newsletters?

7. *Media.* Has the program sought coverage in the newspapers potential volunteers read and the television and radio stations they listen to? Has coverage in other outlets—community and shoppers' newspapers, ethnic radio and television stations—been considered?

8. *Recruitment events.* Has the program held a special volunteer recruitment event, such as a recruitment day or a social evening, when current volunteers are asked to bring a friend who may be interested in volunteering. Do volunteer leaders attend meetings of community organizations or workplace volunteer fairs to recruit volunteers? Has the program considered joining with other nonprofit organizations in a community-wide volunteer recruitment effort?

Responses to these questions can form the outline for a recruitment plan that provides a structure for the recruitment and selection process. The plan should be reviewed periodically and revised according to the needs of the program and the museum.

Sources of Volunteers

Working People

Judging from statistics on the composition of today's volunteer force, a good place to find volunteers is among working people. For some museums, the work force may be the primary focus for recruitment. Working people have much to contribute as museum volunteers; they want opportunities to use their professional skills while spending their leisure time in a meaningful way. Museums must actively respond to their interest by tailoring volunteer jobs and training programs to suit their expertise and by providing convenient evening and weekend schedules. The Denver Art Museum, for example, formed a Museums after Dark council for volunteers who want to work

---

FIGURE 4.2

What Volunteers Value

A group of volunteers connected with a voluntary action center in the Midwest were asked, "How important to you is each of these things in any volunteer job you might have?" Respondents rated each factor on a scale of 1 (not at all important) to 4 (very important).

Rank	Mean Rating on 1-4 Scale
1. Helping others	3.83
2. Clearly defined responsibilities	3.58
3. Interesting work	3.53
4. Competence of immediate supervisor	3.51
5. Supervisor guidance	3.47
6. Seeing results of my work	3.46
7. Working with a respected community organization	3.43
8. Reasonable work schedule	3.41
9. Doing things I do best	3.39
10. Suitable workload	3.22
11. Freedom to decide how to get things done	3.21
12. Chance to make friends	3.20
13. Pleasant physical surroundings	3.17
14. Opportunity to develop special skills/abilities	3.09
15. Challenging problems to solve	3.05
16. Convenient travel to and from volunteer work	2.94
17. Opportunity to work with professional staff	2.88
18. Volunteer recognition	2.49
19. Adequate reimbursement of out-of-pocket expenses	2.07
20. Chance to move to paid employment	1.50

Source: Paul Colomy, Huey-tsyh Chen, and Gregg Andrews, "Situational Facilities and Volunteer Work," *Journal of Volunteer Administration* 20 (Winter 1987-88).

---

on evenings and weekends. Other museums have similar programs (see the Resource Guide).

There are many options for recruiting working people. Some corporations give time off to employees for volunteer projects, although in most cases only for one-time or short-term volunteer projects. Employee associations and unions have the resources to bring out hundreds of volunteers from their membership to staff special events or community service activities; volunteers can also be recruited for such projects through a corporation's public relations or community relations department. Groups ranging from several people to hundreds may be available for a community festival hosted by the museum, maintenance work that requires a crew of people, or a major fund-raising event involving a telephone bank.

It is important to determine whether the organization or corporation plans service projects according to a schedule and to lay the necessary groundwork. Usually, it is wise to request volunteers several months in advance of an event. However, once the museum becomes a favored project, help will be available year after year for recurring needs or events.

Service organizations, fraternal groups, sororities and fraternities, and business and professional organizations also look for volunteer projects. Groups such as Rotary International, Chambers of Commerce, Business and Professional Women USA, and the Junior League have contributed much to museums through-

out the United States. The newest trend is organizations for young professionals who volunteer on weekends for short-term projects.

Most service organizations and fraternal groups have a particular focus, and the museum must assess how its mission fits with that of the organization. For example, an organization such as the Lions Club that works with disabled people may be interested in a project involving accessibility of the museum to disabled visitors. As with business volunteer groups, it is important to know the organization's timetable and criteria for selecting projects and to plan the request accordingly.

People Reentering the Job Market

A source of short-term volunteers is people who want to enter or reenter the job market. For example, students often volunteer to gain work experience that will help them when they graduate. Those in between jobs can also be productively involved. Women who want to return to careers outside the home may want to sharpen their skills before looking for paid employment. University job placement offices, local voluntary action centers, and community agencies or organizations focusing on women's interests are good places to recruit this type of volunteer.

Retired People

Older Americans are the most rapidly growing population group, now num-

FIGURE 4.3

Recruiting Young People as Volunteers

Deborah Edward, director of the Austin (Texas) Children's Museum, offers the following suggestions based on her museum's experience:

1. To recruit young people, use referral systems from youth organizations and library youth volunteer programs.

2. Promote the program's benefits to participants, including workplace skills, experience, and service.

3. Set up the program as an equal partnership between youth, paid staff, and volunteers, and use youth as planners and advisers.

4. Understand the expectations of young volunteers and design a program that meets them.

5. To publicize the program, develop relationships with individuals and businesses that deal with young people, such as school counselors, church groups, and even fast-food outlets. Local business leaders and entertainers can be spokespersons.

6. To fund youth programs, review the Job Partnership Act and look into job training programs for youth.

Source: Deborah McDermott Edward and S. Rodrigues, "Youth Volunteer Programs in Museums" (Austin, TX: Austin Children's Museum, n.d.); Edward, "An Awesome Bunch of Dudes Is Coming to Your Museum," panel presentation at American Association of Museums annual meeting, Chicago, IL, May 1990.

---

bering more than 33 million, and they have vast experience to share as museum volunteers. Retired business executives, scientists, teachers, librarians, museum professionals, and many others may be tremendous assets to a museum. These potential volunteers often register with special nonprofit service organizations; the Retired Senior Volunteer Program (RSVP) and the American Association of Retired Persons (AARP) both have skills banks of retired volunteers. Local volunteer centers help nonprofit organizations recruit retired volunteers. Corporate retiree programs are another good resource.

Most retirees are on fixed incomes, and some may need travel reimbursement. RSVP may help museums support senior volunteers by providing these reimbursements. Museums that have membership requirements for volunteers can lower fees for retired people.

Teachers

Through high school counselors' or teachers' organizations, museums can attract teachers who have special abilities that fit a museum's needs. Teachers and retired teachers are especially able volunteers in educational programs and in behind-the-scenes activities involving collections research. They may also be asked to train other volunteers in areas requiring specialized knowledge.

Young People

Young people make high-energy volunteers. Youth volunteer programs benefit the museum while adding an important dimension to the museum's educational services. By volunteering in such jobs as junior interpreter or behind-the-scenes aide, participants learn in depth about the subject areas of the museum. At the same time, they are introduced to the varied career opportunities available in the museum profession, and some even return as employees to the institutions where they have volunteered. Some high schools encourage students to do community service, and some even have a community service requirement for graduation. The programs vary, but high school seniors may be available for one-semester volunteer projects. High school students may also be interested in summer internships, work-study projects, and paid positions sponsored by community organizations. High shcool counselors and youth organizations are good recruitment sources.

Undergraduate and Graduate Interns

College and university student interns can make significant contributions to activities such as exhibition research or educational program development and often satisfy a degree requirement at the same time. Some graduate internships have stipends, often supported by a grant from a foundation or government agency. Museum internships must be carefully structured so that they are substantive learning experiences for the student; routine office work or visitor services activities are not suitable for internships.

Families

As more and more museums emphasize families as a primary audience, some have experimented with projects engaging families rather than individuals as volunteers. As a result, many parents and children have become devoted volunteers. Mystic Seaport in Connecticut, for instance, recruits families to staff costumed and ticketed events. The volunteer program can work closely with the museum's education and membership departments to let families know about opportunities for volunteer service. Educational programs aimed at a family audience, community events involving the museum, and programs for museum members are especially good avenues for volunteer recruitment.

Disabled People

Disabled people constitute 17 percent of the American population, but due to museums' history of physical inaccessibility, only a small portion of that group are museum-goers. Today, under the Americans with Disabilities Act, people with disabilities have the right of complete access to any program.

The backgrounds and interests of disabled people are just as varied as those of people who are not disabled. Disabled volunteers can contribute a wide range of services in a museum. A primary consideration when recruiting is the physical accessibility of the museum building and grounds. A careful assessment of this issue with advice from disabled people can make the difference between a good volunteer program and one that misses its purpose.

Organizations from which to recruit volunteers and publicize museum programs include:

♦ special education school districts, schools for disabled students, and their parents' organizations

♦ recreational associations and other agencies serving disabled individuals, such as Special Olympics and Very Special Arts

♦ service organizations such as the Lions Club and Easter Seal Association

♦ United Way agencies

♦ advocacy groups and social organizations for disabled people

State branches of the Centers for Independent Living are good resources for identifying organizations from which to recruit volunteers. Sheltered workshops are a source of off-site volunteer assistance. Many have mailing services that handle mass mailings by preparing and folding letters, stuffing envelopes, and sorting them by zip code. Often this service is performed free or for a small charge.

Recruiting a Diverse Volunteer Force

Museums are showing increasing interest in recruiting volunteers who have not traditionally been involved in the museum as volunteers or even as visitors. This important trend must continue if museums are to serve a broader spectrum of our society. The American Association of Museums report, *Excellence and Equity: Education and the Public Dimension of Museums,* underscores the relationship between diversity within the museum and diversity in the museum's audience: "If museums are to be welcoming places for people of different racial, ethnic, social, economic, and educational backgrounds . . . they must recruit, hire or select, and foster the professional growth of trustees, staff, and volunteers who reflect diverse audiences and multiple perspectives."[2]

An active community relations role for the volunteer program is critical to laying the groundwork for recruitment (see "Community Relations," chapter 1). A visible, concerted effort to invite volunteer participation from a particular group or a variety of different groups will pay dividends. A pilot program at the Toledo Museum of Art entailed recruiting and training highly motivated adult volunteers from middle-class minority backgrounds, with little education in art, to lead visitor tours on weekends. A key feature was the use of an advisory council to work with the community and participate actively in program development and implementation.[3]

Recruitment is most effective when tied to museum programming that is aimed at diverse audiences. One of the most appealing and effective ways to recruit a culturally diverse group of volunteers is by enlisting current volunteers who are part of the constituencies you would like to reach and asking them to tell others in their communities about the rewards of volunteering in the museum. Other recruitment avenues include advertising or press coverage through radio stations, television stations, newspapers, and periodicals that reach specific constituencies; flyers posted in local churches, recreation centers, libraries, schools, and businesses; and mailings using lists obtained from ethnic organizations in the community.

An important point to remember is that achieving a culturally diverse volunteer force cannot be accomplished overnight. The process involves confronting stereotypes and changing attitudes—on the part of both the museum's paid staff and current and prospective volunteers. The Association of Junior Leagues International, which has actively sought to meet the challenge of multiculturalism in a historically homogeneous organization, offers the following suggestions, adapted here for museum volunteer programs:

1. *Gain commitment.* Start by gaining the support and commitment of museum leaders and staff. Make sure they see the need for diversity training programs within the organization.

2. *Offer training.* Develop training programs to help volunteers and paid staff develop the skills needed to manage diversity. These programs should help participants come to terms with their own biases; develop listening and problem-solving skills geared to people from other cultures; improve team building and networking skills; learn about the different cultural groups in the community; become adept at cross-cultural communication; and understand stereotyping, prejudice, and racism.

3. *Compile demographic data.* Determine whether you are involving the whole spectrum of your community as volunteers by collecting data on ethnic, age, gender, race, and religious composition. You can find this data through local universities, the city or county planning department, libraries, large nonprofit social service agencies, political organizations, real estate companies, census data, *Sourcebook of Zipcode Demographics* or *REZIDE: The National Encyclopedia of Residential Zipcode Demography,* and the chamber of commerce.

4. *Clarify your vision.* Create a vision for a multicultural volunteer program, and establish goals to attain that dream. Set a tone and develop

an inclusive environment that will support your vision. Evaluate your progress frequently to see if you are meeting your goals. Don't expect a "quick fix." Maintain ongoing commitment.[4]

Using Advisory Groups in Recruitment

An important consideration is whether the museum staff, volunteers, or trustees have the community connections to conduct direct recruitment of volunteers or whether an advisory group of community leaders should be appointed. Teachers and school administrators might advise on how to attract teachers as volunteers in various capacities. Young professionals, perhaps drawn from among the museum's members, can help plan a strategy for recruiting volunteers from their age group. Representatives of organizations serving disabled people are important advisors when seeking disabled volunteers.

Especially when trying to recruit a more diverse group of volunteers, advisory groups representing people the museum wants to reach can help with recruitment, training, and program planning. Volunteer programs that decide to work with advisory groups should cast a wide net in the community and consult a variety of community leaders before appointing group members. Then the volunteer leaders must be prepared to make changes based upon suggestions from the group. Staff, administration, and current volunteers should be wholehearted supporters of this aspect of the recruitment program. Lasting change in the composition of the volunteer force cannot be brought about through short-term efforts. These recruitment efforts need long-term support and constant attention if they are to succeed.

Forming an advisory group must be approached carefully as a special project in its own right. The purpose of the group should be clearly defined. Group members must have some familiarity with the basic mission and environment of the museum. If they do not have this background knowledge, the museum must help them gain it. Advisory group members who are willing to learn, to share their expertise, and to make reasonable suggestions for change will help the volunteer group achieve its goals.

Interviewing and Placing Volunteers

The purpose of the interview is to ascertain the applicant's interests and abilities as they relate to the museum's needs and to see where he or she would best fit in the organization. The success of the volunteer program depends on finding the right person for each volunteer job.

Application Procedures

Prospective volunteers should complete an application form before the interview. The information provided enables the interviewer to learn a few facts about the candidate in advance. Application forms may include the following information:

- ♦ work experience (paid and volunteer)
- ♦ education and training
- ♦ skills, hobbies, and interests
- ♦ availability (weekdays, evenings, or weekends)

The Interview

The setting for the interview should be private and quiet, and the interviewer should make sure there are no interruptions. The interview should include the following steps:

1. Express interest in the applicant and ask a few questions about what is on the application, such as hobbies and work history.

2. Ask about the applicant's interest in volunteering for the museum. What would the applicant like to do?

3. Provide information about the volunteer program in the perceived area of interest, along with descriptions of some exciting new programs or options.

4. Give details about a particular job or several jobs that seem to be interesting to the volunteer, with information about the time commitment, training schedule, and the museum's expectations. Provide written job descriptions. If the prospective volunteer cannot de-

cide on a specific job, invite him or her to observe the program or attend a meeting before deciding.

5. Explain the museum's volunteer policy and benefits.

6. Thank the candidate at the end of the interview, and let him or her know you will be in touch, specifying when.

7. Immediately after the interview, write a brief summary of the conversation and record your impressions of the candidate.

The initial interviews usually are conducted by the volunteer administrator. In some museums candidates are also interviewed by the staff supervisor in the department where they would be working. These interviews can reveal gaps in the candidate's knowledge and determine whether his or her skills and personal qualities are a good match with the department's needs. Some museums use a team of paid staff and experienced volunteers for interviewing. If a variety of interviewers is used, however, it is important to maintain consistency in conducting the interviews and evaluating candidates.

Whatever the method, the interview stage is extremely important. An effective interview can probe the candidate's true interests and lead to a job well suited to his or her skills. Sometimes the prospective volunteer has a preconceived notion of what he or she would like to do in the museum, but in the course of the interview it becomes apparent that another

FIGURE
4.4

Volunteer Questionnaire

Natural History Museum of Los Angeles County

Please take a few minutes to fill out this questionnaire. We would like to utilize your time and skills effectively—while ensuring you will enjoy your activities.

_____
Name

_____
Address

_____
City / State / Zip

_____
Phone / Date available

Which days would you like to work? (please circle)   M   T   W   Th   F

Would you prefer to work in the morning or afternoon?   AM   PM

Do you have office experience?

☐ Yes   ☐ No

If yes, does that experience include

☐ Answering phones/taking messages

☐ Bookkeeping

☐ Filing

☐ Taking dictation

☐ Typing   (wpm) _____

☐ Writing letters/memos

Do you have computer experience?

☐ Yes   ☐ No

If yes, please indicate the software you have used:

_____

If no, would you be interested in learning to use computers?   ☐ Yes   ☐ No

Do you speak any language(s) other than English?   ☐ Yes   ☐ No

If yes, which?

_____

Please check any areas of our collections in which you have studied or have special interest:

☐ Anthropology

☐ Botany

☐ Education

☐ Entomology

☐ Herpatology

☐ History (General Americana)

☐ History (Transportation & Communication)

☐ History (Western Research)

☐ Ichthyology

☐ Invertebrate Paleontology

☐ Invertabrate Zoology (Crustacea)

☐ Invertabrate Zoology (Echinoderms)

☐ Invertabrate Zoology (Polycheates)

☐ Invertabrate Zoology (Malacology)

☐ Library

☐ Mammalogy

☐ Mineralogy

☐ Ornithology

☐ Vertebrate Paleontology

List any experience and/or special skills that you bring to us!

_____

_____

Which type of project do you prefer?

☐ Long term projects, ie: several weeks

☐ Short term projects, ie: a few hours

Are there projects you would like to avoid? ☐ Yes ☐ No

If yes, please list. _____

_____

Would you be available for "physical labor", ie: moving crates, tables, wall panels? ☐ Yes ☐ No

Do you find any of the following easy and/or fun to do?

☐ Data entry

☐ Organizing large quantities of information into a file or database system

☐ Proofing correspondence, contracts, manuscripts and/or lists

☐ Researching special projects

☐ Spelling (especially scientific terms)

☐ Editing

Do you have previous museum experience? ☐ Yes ☐ No

If yes, where have you worked and in what capacity?

_____

_____

Source: Natural History Museum
of Los Angeles County
900 Exposition Boulevard
Los Angeles, CA 90007
(213) 744-2414

job will be more appropriate and rewarding for the volunteer and the museum. Volunteer administrators should never press a prospective volunteer into an agreement. If the volunteer and the job are poorly matched, the volunteer will not be able to sustain a commitment to it.

If the candidate is accepted, he or she should promptly receive a letter of confirmation and further information about the program and the museum, along with a schedule of orientation and training meetings. A volunteer service agreement can be used to formalize the relationship (Figure 4.5). Sometimes the guidelines set forth in volunteer policy are enough. If the candidate is not accepted, send a letter of appreciation for his or her time or interest; include a guest pass to the museum. If possible, suggest some other volunteer opportunities for which the candidate is better suited.

Finding volunteers who are eager to put their skills to work for the museum is just the beginning. If the museum and its visitors are to receive the full benefit of the enthusiasm, commitment, and expertise of its volunteers, recruitment and selection must be followed by a comprehensive training, continuing education, and appreciation for their contributions.

FIGURE 4.5

Volunteer Agreements

The San Jose Historical Museum

The San Jose (California) Historical Museum gives volunteers the following statement of "Volunteer Philosophy":

As the Museum, we will provide for you:

♦ An interesting opportunity to provide public service at a museum.

♦ Professional orientation and training.

♦ A supportive climate where volunteers can perform and grow.

♦ Meaningful, necessary tasks to be done.

♦ Recognition and reaffirmation of individual's worth.

♦ Opportunity for new friendships.

♦ A chance to serve the community.

♦ An opportunity to promote the history of San Jose.

As a volunteer we ask you to:

♦ Choose an assignment appropriate to your interests, abilities and time.

♦ Participate in a prescribed training program.

♦ Establish a regular schedule (minimum of 6 hours per month).

♦ Commit to one year service to San Jose Historical Museum.

♦ Observe time schedule.

♦ Follow prescribed procedures of job performance, including changes.

♦ Notify the Museum when you have arranged for a substitute.

♦ Share in evaluations.

♦ Serve three months' provisional status.

♦ Read *Volunteer* and *Association* newsletters.

♦ Participate in continuing education.

♦ Serve as a "goodwill ambassador" for the Museum.

♦ Belong to San Jose Historical Museum Association (our nonprofit support organization).

♦ Enjoy yourself and let us know how to better our volunteer programs.

San Jose Historical Museum
635 Phelen Avenue
San Jose, CA 95112
(408) 287-2290

Volunteer Agreements
Conner Prairie Pioneer Settlement

At Conner Prairie Pioneer Settlement in Noblesville, Indiana, the volunteer and the volunteer coordinator agree in writing to their responsibilities.

Volunteer/Staff Agreement

The *volunteer* agrees:

♦ to work a determined number of hours according to a schedule acceptable to Conner Prairie

♦ to become familiar with the policies and procedures (written and verbal) set forth by Conner Prairie

♦ to be prompt and reliable in reporting for assignment

♦ to provide Conner Prairie with an accurate record of hours

♦ to notify the Coordinator/Department supervisor as early as possible if unable to report or find a replacement

♦ to notify Coordinator of replacement's name & phone number

♦ to attend training sessions and undertake additional education if necessary to retain competence

♦ to inform Coordinator in writing, at least three weeks in advance, of resignation or leave of absence

♦ to return volunteer manual upon resignation

♦ to understand that irregular attendance, poor performance, or failure to cooperate with Conner Prairie policies may be interpreted as a volunteer's desire to resign

The *staff supervisor* agrees:

♦ to provide adequate training

♦ to provide adequate supervision

♦ to be available to discuss problems, ideas, or suggestions

♦ to understand a volunteer's absence in an emergency

♦ to respect the function of the volunteer and to contribute to a smooth working relationship between staff and volunteers

The *volunteer coordinator* agrees:

♦ to act as a liaison between volunteers and staff

♦ to assist in planning training programs

♦ to be available to discuss ideas, suggestions, or problems

♦ to assist volunteers in evaluating their assignments and making necessary changes

♦ to plan yearly activities to include Orientation and recognition

♦ to keep volunteers and staff informed throughout the year by special mailings, newsletters, etc.

_____
Volunteer   Date

_____
Volunteer Coordinator   Date

Conner Prairie Pioneer Settlement
P.O. Box 50605
Indianapolis, IN 46250
(317) 776-6000

5

INSPIRING EFFECTIVENESS

TRAINING, PROFESSIONAL DEVELOPMENT AND RECOGNITION OF VOLUNTEERS

Every volunteer must understand the relationship of his or her work to the public service the institution provides. Volunteers need training that informs them about the museum and prepares them for specific jobs; opportunities for continuing professional growth and development; and recognition for a job well done. With such an understanding, the volunteer's commitment is strengthened, and the result is a satisfying experience for the volunteer, a significant contribution to the museum, and a true service to the public.

Museums generally provide four types of training for volunteers: orientation to the museum and the volunteer program, general training regarding volunteer responsibilities, specialized training to carry out volunteer jobs and advanced training opportunities, including management training for leadership volunteers or continuing education in area of specialization

Orientation and general training can be combined in a two-part, full-day session. The participants' schedules, as well as the amount of specialized training that will follow these introductory programs, will dictate the amount of time to be devoted to each type of training.

Planning a Training Curriculum

The first step in planning training sessions is to identify the audience. For orientation or general training, participants will generally be new or returning volunteers; occasionally paid staff supervisors or current volunteers who would like a refresher session will attend. The audience for a specialized training program may be diverse, including new volunteers, current volunteers who are training for a new position, or returning

volunteers who need to brush up on their skills and learn about new developments in their work areas. Advanced training is offered for an experienced audience focused on a special purpose, including current volunteers, leadership volunteers, and volunteer committee chairs.

Once the audience has been determined, the content, methodology, and logistics can be developed according to the following guidelines:

1. *Specify the learning objectives.* What should volunteers gain from the experience—information, skills, attitude change? How will they be able to use this training for the long-range benefit of the museum?

2. *Ascertain the probable size of the group.* Group size will influence curriculum content, teaching methodology, and logistics.

3. *Identify curriculum content.* What topics should be covered to achieve the learning objectives? What are some alternative plans for addressing these topics?

4. *Anticipate the volunteers' expectations for the training session.* What knowledge or skills do they want to gain, and how do they want to participate as learners?

5. *Decide on a format.* Should there be one session or a series? large or small groups? participatory activities or a more formal lecture-and-discussion approach?

6. *Determine who else should be involved.* Is it appropriate to engage supervisors, curators, the director, the president of the volunteer council, a board member, or guest experts?

7. *List the materials needed.* Reading lists, case studies, worksheets, forms, audio-visuals, and charts may need to be assembled, and tours or demonstrations may need to be organized.

8. *Create an inventive title.* Choose a title that is both appealing and descriptive.

9. *Select a date, time, and location.* The schedule should be convenient for both volunteers and training session faculty. The meeting space should accommodate the group comfortably and provide an atmosphere conducive to learning.

The content and methodology of the training curriculum should be tailored to the objectives of the session and the needs of the participants. Educators believe that, for adults, interactive methods—such as role playing, small group activities, demonstrations, and panel discussions with ample audience participation—are more successful than a lecture format. Educators also know that people have a variety of learning styles. The curriculum and pace of activity should be flexible enough to accommodate the different experiences, needs, and abilities of the participants. The curriculum should also be revised periodically so that volunteers returning for a refresher session will be stimulated and challenged by new information.

The logistics of the training program, too, should be tailored to the volunteers. Museums often recruit volunteers who have paid jobs during the day and want flexible weekend and evening schedules at the museum. Training for these volunteers should take into account their schedules and their expertise. The training sessions should be held on evenings or weekends. Materials should be accessible to volunteers who cannot use the museum library during the day. Some museums provide photocopies or choose materials that are available at public or university libraries during weekend and evening hours. Often, volunteers themselves are the best source of expertise and should be included as presenters in the training session. A librarian who is volunteering to work in the museum's library or archives, for example, can draw on a wealth of experience that will enrich the discussion.

Volunteer Manual

The volunteer manual is an essential guide to the policies and procedures of the museum and the volunteer program. When introduced during training, it becomes an indispensable resource to volunteers.

The volunteer manual should include:

FIGURE 5.1

Sample Volunteer Fact Sheet

Welcome to the Registrar's Office. We are pleased that you have chosen to work with us on the important projects carried out by our office. Our volunteers contribute significantly to our ability to meet deadlines and perform the mission of our Museum. This sheet is designed to answer some of the questions you may have about our office. If you have other questions, please ask.

Volunteer Badge/Photograph

The photography department is available on Thursday mornings (with an appointment) to take a photograph for your volunteer badge. When you show this badge to the parking attendants and guards at the staff entrance, it will simplify your sign-in/sign-out procedure.

Soon after you arrive, your picture will also be taken by someone in the Registrar's Office for our Special Recognition Board. These photographs introduce you to other Museum employees.

Sign-in

Our volunteer coordinator has asked us to track how many hours you work in the Registrar's Office. This important information is incorporated into numerous reports and grant applications so your cooperation is greatly appreciated. The log is kept next to the Recognition Board.

Scheduling

Volunteer hours in our office are completely flexible to accommodate your schedule. While most volunteers prefer to have a set time to come, others prefer to keep their work schedules open. In order to make certain that we have projects lined up for you, we encourage you to let us know when to expect you so we can fill in the volunteer calendar.

Special Assignments

You will be given a section in the volunteer file cabinet for your projects. You may

♦ Welcoming statement describing the purpose of the manual

♦ Brief overview of the museum and the volunteer program, including a description of the audience the museum serves (or would like to serve)

♦ Rewards and benefits of volunteering in the museum

♦ Annual calendar of volunteer activities, training sessions, for volunteers, including dates, times, and locations if available; tours; required meetings; and special events

♦ Requirements and procedures for volunteers, including provisional status, training, membership (volunteer organization and museum), minimum hours, absences, emergency procedures, resignation, evaluation, grounds for dismissal, appeal process, inactive status

♦ Statement of professional standards and ethics for volunteers

use this area to keep your unfinished projects in until the job is complete. It is a good idea to check the drawer each time you arrive to see if special assignments have been placed there for you.

Lunch/Refreshments

Coffee and bottled water are available in our kitchen. Please help yourself. For the safety of our documents, these beverages should remain in the kitchen.

We also have a refrigerator where you may store your lunch. We normally bring our lunch and eat it on the patio or in the cafeteria. We hope that you will feel free to join us. We love to hear about your exciting trips and adventures. Even though this is a natural history museum, we do not want to collect critters in the Registrar's Office, so we are careful not to leave food in our trash cans.

Office Supplies

Our office will provide you with any necessary supplies to complete a project. Many volunteers share the work stations so, if you do not find the items you require in the cabinet drawers beside your table,

please let us know so we can order them from the supply room.

Document Locations

Our office provides many important services to museum staff. Throughout the day, curators and collection managers visit our office requesting collection/donor information. You may be asked to help them find information.

Naturally, we give you a tour of the office when you begin and later you work with many of the documents. When staff members request assistance in locating documents, many times you can locate them by referring to the color-coded map located next to the light switch in the central office. However, our numbering system is on the complicated side, so feel free to ask us to assist you.

Thanks again for your participation.

Source: Natural History Museum
of Los Angeles County
900 Exposition Boulevard
Los Angeles, CA 90007
(213) 744-2414

- ♦ Sample evaluation forms (staff, self-evaluation, program evaluation)

- ♦ Service record forms and instructions

- ♦ Fact sheet about the volunteer organization's history, structure, and programs, including brief descriptions of each volunteer activity and a list of current officers; information about other volunteer organizations in the museum

- ♦ Fact sheet about the museum, including history, collections, programs, and exhibitions

- ♦ General information about the museum's facilities

- ♦ List of museum staff, titles, and phone numbers

The volunteer manual should be well organized and concisely written. It should familiarize volunteers with the museum and the volunteer program but not overwhelm them with too much information. A looseleaf format is useful because volunteers can update the manual and add material relevant to their own job assignments.

Orientation

All new volunteers—as well as former volunteers who are returning to the museum—should be required to attend a basic orientation session that introduces them to the museum and the volunteer program. Current volunteers should also be encouraged to attend orientation sessions periodically to refresh their knowledge. Orientation welcomes volunteers to the museum and acquaints them with its mission, organizational structure, programs, policies, and procedures. An institution with a number of volunteer groups may make the orientation program an opportunity to welcome all incoming or returning volunteers together.

The volunteer administrator, a senior volunteer, and key staff conduct the session. The following topics should be covered:

- History and overview of the museum, including discussion of mission and goals, sources of financial support (including the vital role of volunteers), educational role in the community, and organizational structure

- History and highlights of the collection

- Description of the audience the museum serves and those it would like to serve better

- Overview of current and upcoming exhibitions and programs

- General discussion of volunteers' role in the museum and in the community on behalf of the museum

- Benefits of volunteering

- Policies and procedures of the museum

- Question-and-answer period

- Tour led by docents and paid staff, including areas not generally open to the public

The orientation session should emphasize how much the museum values the volunteer program and what volunteers have accomplished. The museum director should welcome new volunteers and express appreciation on behalf of the staff for their work at the museum.

General Training

In addition to orientation, all new volunteers should be required to attend a comprehensive general training course. This training provides an in-depth introduction to the museum's mission of public service and educates volunteers about their roles and responsibilities. This training should address the following topics:

- Comprehensive discussion of the museum's public service functions in such areas as exhibitions, interpretive programs, research, collections care and management, community relations, school programs, and visitor services.

♦ Volunteer opportunities in each of these areas

♦ Role of volunteers in relation to paid staff

♦ Mission, policies, and procedures of the volunteer program

♦ Procedures for individual and program evaluation

♦ Opportunities for advancement to higher competency levels and more challenging jobs and for retreat to less active jobs if needed

The comprehensive training course should be led by the volunteer administrator, paid staff who work with volunteers, and experienced volunteers.

Communication Skills

A critical aspect of volunteer training is acquiring and practicing skills and techniques for communicating with visitors. The public service aspect of a volunteer's job cannot be overemphasized; public service should be the underlying theme of all volunteer training. Museums serve visitors from a variety of ages, interests, backgrounds, and level of comfort with museum-going. Information about audience characteristics helps volunteers learn about the visitors they will meet and tailor their approach to visitors' needs.

Communication skills are especially necessary for volunteers in interpretive programs, visitor services, fund raising and special events, and community relations. But behind-the-scenes volunteers may also be involved with the public, too—if they respond to telephone inquiries or assist researchers, for example. Communication skills can be addressed in specialized training sessions, but the topic should be introduced in the general training program because it is so important to volunteers' success. The Smithsonian Institution, for example, conducts a special session as part of initial training activities for volunteer information specialists that addresses sensitivity issues in working with multicultural, physically disabled, mentally challenged, and elderly audiences.

Specialized Training

Every volunteer position requires specialized training, some more extensive than others. Docents or interpretive specialists, for example—who must have comprehensive knowledge of specific subjects—usually are required to participate in a formal training program that may last a year or more.

The key to success is training by experts—staff supervisors and others—who are well versed in the area of volunteer responsibility and commitment. Outside authorities can also be brought in; independent conservators, for instance, can train volunteers in collections care and handling. Another useful

FIGURE 5.2 — The Top 25 Methods to Retain Volunteers

25. Each of us has our own unique motivators. If you really want a volunteer to stay, learn what motivates that person and then put that information into practice.

24. Successfully place the volunteer in the beginning. If you place a volunteer in a position that maximizes their potential for success, logic says that they will succeed. And successful people tend to be happy people and happy people tend to stay.

23. If your agency doesn't already have one, hire a professional Volunteer Program Administrator.

22. Don't be afraid of saying "Thank You" too much. I've never heard of a volunteer quitting because they felt over appreciated. Over worked, yes! Over appreciated, no!

21. Vary your recognition program. The same old banquet every year with the same old rewards gets boring. When a volunteer stops attending because they've already re-papered their house in certificates of appreciation, you know it's time to move on to something new.

20. Take the time to train the volunteer so that they know what they need to know in order to do their job.

19. For absolutely no reason at all, send the volunteer a note just to say "hi. "

18. Once a year, ask the volunteers to give an anonymous evaluation of the agency, the paid staff, and the programs (including the volunteer program).

17. Promote volunteers to new positions that require new skills, additional training, and added commitment. Just because Dan is great at stuffing envelopes, doesn't mean that he is going to be happy doing it for the next ten years.

16. Acknowledge that the agency is not your volunteer's number one priority in life. Guilt may have worked for your parents, but it doesn't work with volunteers.

15. Don't call the same volunteers over and over again. It's too easy to become dependent on the "Yes" people and burn them out. You also miss out on developing a new pool of talent.

14. Use the media to promote your active volunteers. The media just loves stories about volunteers; next to all the depressing headlines, these stories create a nice balance. Plus, no matter what they say, people just love to see their name in print.

technique is a mentor system in which experienced volunteers work alongside new volunteers to monitor their progress and offer practical advice and constructive criticism.

Volunteers must learn the subject matter, skills, and procedures they need to do the job. The training should involve observation and participation, with new volunteers being given frequent oppor-

13. Begin a Volunteer Advisory Committee. (Please note: the key word is "Advisory") Such committees help to empower the volunteers, giving them a stronger connection to the agency and its mission, and a reason to stay involved.

12. Practice the fine art of informal evaluations. It's amazing how much feedback you can get by just chatting with your volunteers.

11. Resist the urge to "play favorites." In other words, be consistent with your policies.

10. Always emphasize your agency's mission statement. People no longer volunteer for agencies, they volunteer for causes.

9. Be flexible as an agency.

8. Be flexible as an individual.

7. Smile. No matter how much you want to grab the computer terminal and throw it across the room, don't let it show. Never let them see your stress.

6. Make the volunteer environment at your agency fun. No matter what work the volunteers are doing, they should have a good time doing it.

5. Set limitations with the paid staff. If the Operations Manager suggests that they use volunteers to clean up at the annual "Farm Animal and Petting Zoo Fundraiser," just say "No!" Your volunteers are too valuable to be given the tasks that nobody else wants to do.

4. Every once in a while, work alongside your volunteers. Give them the sense of teamwork and the knowledge that you won't ask them to do anything that you wouldn't do yourself.

3. Consider your volunteers as Unpaid Staff and include them whenever possible in office parties, lottery pools, etc.

2. Be sure to balance the needs of the agency with the needs of your volunteers. Remember, it has to be a mutually satisfying relationship for both parties.

And the number one method for retaining volunteers—drum roll, please—

1. Convince the entire paid staff to follow rules 2 through 25 because one person can't do it alone. Volunteer programs only work with a commitment that starts at the very top of the organization and continues all the way down through each successive level.

Source: Excerpted from a presentation by John L. Lipp at the annual conference of the Museum Association of Arizona, Tucson, 1992. The presentation was part of a panel entitled "Volunteers! Now That You've Got Them, How Do You Get Them to Stay?"

tunities to watch experienced volunteers at work and to practice what they are learning. Training materials should be thorough and clearly presented. Throughout the training course, the emphasis should be on professionalism. Volunteers should know that the course itself is the foundation for continuing education; they should be encouraged to improve their knowledge and skills throughout their volunteer service.

The areas to be addressed in training sessions will vary from job to job. Volunteers who work at the visitor services desk need to know the museum inside and out, from the location of the restrooms to the details of current exhibitions to the reason the exhibition in Gallery A is no longer on view. Museum store volunteers need extensive knowledge of the shop's merchandise and how it relates to the museum's mission and collections; techniques for explaining merchandise to customers; and sales procedures such as operating equipment, handling money, and making daily reports. Volunteers who work behind the scenes with the collections must be able to put the objects in historic, artistic, or scientific context. They must understand the professional standards and ethical and legal guidelines applicable to their assignment, and they need specific technical skills such as how to handle, clean, or label objects. Interpretive program volunteers require in-depth knowledge of the subject matter; understanding of the variety of learning styles; teaching and communication skills; and familiarity with the organizational structure, procedures, and programs of the education department. Many volunteers will benefit from training in working with disabled visitors (Figure 5.3).

Advanced Training

Volunteer training does not end with the formal training sessions. The most effective volunteers are those who are involved in and informed about matters related to their individual volunteer assignments and the museum as a whole. Museums use a variety of techniques to make sure that volunteers have current information. These techniques include:

♦ regular training and enrichment meetings for small groups of volunteers

♦ volunteer day captains who are responsible for updating volunteers on current events and providing timely information about the museum's programs and activities

♦ periodic volunteer manual updates

♦ a newsletter for volunteers

Advanced training enhances the skills of experienced and long-term volunteers who show talent in leadership. Formal sessions can involve outside trainers from corporations, voluntary action centers, or professional organizations. Examples of areas in which advanced training can be offered are:

♦ team building and the team approach to project development

♦ training the trainer

♦ developing a resumé or curriculum vitae for the volunteer

Working With Disabled Visitors

FIGURE
5.3

Training about accessibility for disabled visitors is recommended for all volunteers and paid staff, not just those who will work directly with these visitors. Training program topics can include:

♦ using museum materials and audio-visual equipment to the best advantage of disabled visitors

♦ preparing paid staff and volunteers to handle emergencies involving disabled visitors

♦ recognizing and working with the various aids that disabled people use

♦ understanding specific techniques for working with visitors with different disabilities

♦ developing communication skills for working with disabled visitors

In addition to these general topics, specialized training can include

♦ planning accessible museum tours

♦ conducting specific programs (such as helping the visually impaired handle objects)

An advisory council involving disabled people can help training session planners become familiar with issues and problems that are important to disabled visitors. Disabled staff members can also facilitate training program design.

Source: Janice Majewski
Accessibility Coordinator
Smithsonian Institution

♦ enhancing presentation skills

♦ interviewing and placing volunteers

Leadership volunteers benefit from lunchtime sessions at which they hear a presentation by an outside trainer or a staff member. These sessions may also serve as means of acquainting volunteers with paid staff. Another way of providing such training is to ask the volunteer to attend, with paid staff, conferences of national, regional, and state museum associations or associations of volunteer administrators.

Field trips are another form of advanced or enrichment training for experienced volunteers. These trips should be consistent with the missions of the museum and the volunteer organization and should be planned in conjunction with one or more museum department.

Tours may range from one-day programs to weeklong tours. By visiting another museum or related facility or going on tours led by another museum's volunteers, volunteers can learn more about such facets of museums as exhibit design and installation, collections management, and research. Tours can focus on behind-the-scenes views of artists' studios, private collections, or related institutions.

Volunteer Recognition

The most effective way to show appreciation to volunteers is to recognize that every volunteer who makes a commitment and fulfills it is valuable to the museum and to the public. Whether that recognition comes in the form of a heartfelt thank-you or a framed certificate depends on the museum, the volunteer program, and the individual volunteer. Having a recognition plan that lists informal and formal recognition activities is a good way to ensure that this important aspect of administering a volunteer program is given appropriate emphasis (Figure 5.4).

The best informal recognition of volunteers is a supportive atmosphere in which volunteers are contributing members of a team whose goal is public service. Promotion to a more responsible position is another form of recognition, although not every volunteer wants more responsibility or has the ability to assume it. It is important, too, to treat volunteers as professionals by involving them in staff meetings and planning sessions that affect their work or providing advanced training in their areas of specialization. Personal gestures are meaningful: remembering names, saying thank-you at the end of the day, asking about children and grandchildren, and sending notes of thanks at the end of a project, after a volunteer has served a certain number of hours, or, even better, when there is no particular occasion. One museum director circulates through the museum once a day to thank volunteers who are on duty. Such efforts on the part of museum administration go a long

FIGURE 5.4

When and Where to Recognize Volunteers

When:

1. At the time they sign up to volunteer (send a welcome letter)

2. Daily or weekly (informal thank-yous and praise)

3. Monthly (volunteer of the month, newsletter articles)

4. Annually (annual banquet or volunteer appreciation day)

5. At the completion of a special project

6. On their birthdays or other holidays

7. When they are sick

8. At the time they leave

9. During National Volunteer Week

Where:

1. Agency bulletin board or newsletter

2. At home

3. At their place of employment

4. In the media

5. Anywhere people they know will see it

FIGURE
5.5

Special Benefits for Volunteers

Here are some of the benefits museums offer volunteers:

♦ free catalogues and exhibition information

♦ special exhibition previews

♦ discounts on museum memberships and purchases at the museum shop and restaurant

♦ privileges such as use of the museum library or the staff dining room

♦ special visits to other museums

♦ free or discounted admission to lectures, concerts, films, and other public events at the museum

♦ reimbursement for transportation and lunch expenses (for retired people and other special groups)

♦ reciprocal admission to other museums with presentation of volunteer card

♦ special courses and lectures for volunteers only

♦ social events for volunteers

way toward helping volunteers feel satisfied and rewarded.

There are many other ways to recognize volunteers for their service. Giving pins for five, ten and twenty-five years' service, certificates, or gifts at volunteer recognition events is one means. An award can honor the individual while giving value to the museum—a book donated to the museum library in the name of the award recipient, for example. National Volunteer Week, an annual observance each April, can be the focal point for recognition events. A range of special benefits can be reserved for volunteers (see Figure 5.5).

When volunteer training is of high quality and when volunteers receive appreciation and recognition for jobs well done, everyone benefits. The volunteer approaches his or her assignment equipped with knowledge, skills, confidence, and enthusiasm. The museum has high-caliber individuals who are committed to providing the very best public service. And the visitor encounters informed, cordial volunteers who help make the museum an inviting, welcoming place. When there is a productive, collegial relationship between paid and unpaid staff, the benefits are even greater.

COMMUNICATING WITH ONE ANOTHER

VOLUNTEER-STAFF
RELATIONS

An effective volunteer program requires the sound foundation of a mutually respectful relationship between volunteers and paid staff. Establishing and maintaining a relationship in which communication is open and productive can be a challenge in some museums, especially when there has been a tradition of competition rather than teamwork. Successful volunteer programs are driven by a spirit of collabora-tion and by the understanding that everyone—volunteer and paid staff alike—brings valuable qualities to the shared task of public service.

Good volunteer-staff relations require an investment of time and attention. Volunteers and paid staff need to understand the organizational climate or climates in which they work and the perceptions they have of one another. The museum must provide appropriate training in volunteer administration for staff supervisors. Volunteers and staff together must strive for open, two-way communication within the organizational structure. Volunteers must remember that staff supervisors have many demands on their time, and they must respect the professional expertise of staff members. Conversely, staff supervisors must be aware of specific time commitments volunteers have made and work within those commitments. And finally, volunteers must observe the same standards of professional practice as their colleagues on the museum staff.

Assessing Perceptions and Organizational Climate

In their day-to-day working relationships, paid staff and volunteers sometimes forget that they are a part of one organization. Staff and volunteer leadership perceptions of one another affect the way they relate in the workplace. Neither has unrealistic expectations, but, the key to a successful relationship is a mutual effort to meet those expectations (see Figure 6.1).

The organizational climate of the museum and the management styles of the volunteer administrator, volunteer supervisors, and volunteer leaders help define the working relationship between staff and volunteers and ultimately determine the success of the volunteer program. Within any one museum, different organizational climates can be present in different departments.

The best working environment is an open climate that meets volunteers' social needs and at the same time encourages efficiency. In this climate decision making is democratic, and communication flows two ways. Volunteers have a voice in planning and in any decisions that affect them. Instead of having to conform automatically to written rules, volunteers are led to understand and accept the guidelines set out for them. They accept the structure and leadership of the organization and do not threaten the function and authority of paid staff. A high level of trust and mutual respect develops; relationships between paid staff and volunteers are friendly and supportive.

The role of the volunteer administrator or staff supervisor in an open climate is that of an athletic coach who stimulates teamwork and provides support and encouragement that sustain morale and productivity. The supervisor also acts as a diagnostician, finding out what is wrong, giving constructive feedback, and helping to correct problems in a professional way. The supervisor cares about the volunteers and delegates a significant amount of decision making to them. New recruits are immediately welcomed into the group. They are trained thoroughly and become devoted to the mission of the organization. In an open climate morale is usually high, so volunteers are naturally productive. Both volunteers and paid staff receive recognition for their contributions to the museum.

How Volunteers and Supervisors Perceive One Another

FIGURE 6.1

Results of a 1987 AAMV Survey

In the eyes of volunteers, staff supervisors should:

♦ Explain why things are done.

♦ Be clear about what is expected.

♦ Learn the skill of supervising volunteers; learn how to attract and keep volunteers.

♦ Improve communication skills with volunteers and with other staff.

♦ Alert volunteer leaders or administrator to problems as well as to exceptional work.

♦ Practice positive feedback and rewards, make rewards meaningful, and make volunteers feel important.

♦ Keep volunteers current on museum programs and policy changes.

♦ Recognize volunteers as professionals and treat them as such.

♦ Set minimum hours and steady time for volunteers.

♦ Learn how to use and train management-level volunteers.

♦ Recognize the limitations that volunteers have on their time because of personal commitments.

♦ Realize that volunteers have social needs.

In the eyes of staff supervisors, volunteers should:

♦ Respect museum rules as professional standards rather than as obstacles.

♦ Be open to change, new ideas, and restructuring.

♦ Know their job descriptions.

♦ Provide status reports or messages on a regular basis.

♦ Have another option to offer when they come to the staff with a problem or criticism.

♦ Be honest about what they can and cannot do and what they do and do not want to do.

♦ Inform the staff of volunteer plans, activities, decisions, and concerns.

♦ Consider themselves professionals and conduct themselves accordingly.

♦ Be aware of the extreme importance of time: Don't steal it or waste it, but always take it.

♦ Consider the staff's schedules: that staff meeting days are always hectic, that institutional deadlines can interfere with the best of intentions, and that 9 AM and 4:30 PM are not good times for conversation.

♦ Recognize that the staff, too, needs support, recognition, and praise.

Attention to organizational climate and management style can make a great difference in the morale and productivity of volunteers. When problems arise, it may be productive to examine the organizational climates and management styles present in the museum or department in question, before volunteers are blamed for poor service.

There are potential barriers to good relationships between volunteers and staff. Lines of communication must always remain open in regard to such matters as program structure, reporting systems, training, and evaluation. It takes time and effort to build systems of communication, define and discuss shared goals and values for the museum's public service, and ensure that both volunteers and paid staff understand their shared stake in the success of the museum.

Improving Communication

Paid staff and volunteers sometimes consider one another to be intrusions: Staff members view supervising volunteers as yet another demand on their time and feel that they have no recourse if the quality of a volunteer's work is inadequate. Volunteers adopt the mind-set that because they are not being paid for their work they are not accountable for their actions; long-time volunteer leaders sometimes resist what they consider to be intrusions from staff. To ensure that these perceptions are not permitted to dominate the volunteer program—and detract from the significant contributions volunteers can make—an open system of two-way communication is essential.

Staff supervisors should make every effort to work through the volunteer leadership. Such a collaborative approach is especially fruitful when staff

want to effect change. So that volunteers will understand the basis for change in a familiar program, staff members should consult with volunteer leaders or committee chairs. When volunteers are given examples and options to evaluate and consider, change becomes a shared goal rather than an edict issued by staff. Volunteer administrators and staff supervisors can encourage volunteers to contribute their ideas by enabling them to meet with volunteers from other museums with well-run programs to gather ideas, share information, and develop a network of support. The staff can also collect resources and reading material. In many cities, "roundtable" organizations of volunteer administrators, paid and unpaid, from a variety of cultural institutions including museums, orchestras, zoos, botanical gardens, and public television stations provide mutual support, stimulate ideas, and promote collaboration both within and among institutions. When staff and volunteers attend such meetings together, a sense of shared participation in institutional mission is enhanced.

A formal way of encouraging teamwork is to create a staff-volunteer task force as a forum for exchanging ideas and information on communications issues. It will take time—a year or more is not too much to expect—to develop the right communications structure, but the time will be well spent. The task force's work will strengthen a long-range planning process, create a sense of shared values, and help volunteers and staff form bonds of mutual respect. Throughout the process, task force members should remain focused on their common purpose: to help the museum function more effectively so that it can better serve its public.

Another way to stimulate cooperation and mutual respect is to assure that the museum's long-range plan, which establishes goals and objectives for the institution, encompasses the goals and objectives of the volunteer program. The plan should recognize volunteer contributions to every aspect of the museum, not just in terms of hours but in terms of real jobs and goals that volunteers are expected to achieve. When the volunteer program is a vital part of institutional planning, it gains the respect of the board, the administration, the paid staff, and the volunteers themselves. The integration of volunteer activities into the long-range plan makes it clear that everyone is working to accomplish the same mission.

Staff and volunteers can also stimulate communication on a daily basis. By making a point of listening to suggestions from volunteer leaders for improving the management of volunteers, staff members set positive examples of open communication. Often the best ideas come from volunteers who see new opportunities for their peers within the museum or propose better ways of doing things. The most thoughtful and articulate volunteers frequently will be the next volunteer leaders. Consequently, encouraging suggestions and providing an open forum for the discussion of needed changes will benefit the museum

in developing future volunteer leadership.

Reporting systems need to allow and encourage communication in both directions; paid staff should keep volunteers informed about current and future museum exhibitions, programs, and other activities, and volunteers should let the staff know about projects they would like to be involved in. Volunteer programs should adopt the same systems for planning, budgeting, and public relations that are in place for paid staff. Operating the volunteer organization within the same structure as all museum departments reinforces the notion that volunteers are unpaid staff and underscores their commitment to teamwork and communication.

The organization should conduct its own annual evaluation (see chapter 7). If it fails to face its problems as a group or confront volunteers who are not meeting established standards, the program devalues itself and the work of individual volunteers. As a result, paid staff will have diminished respect for the volunteer program and for the important contributions volunteers make to the museum.

Providing Training for Supervisors

Volunteers are unpaid staff. If the museum accepts this premise, then volunteer administration should be incorporated in the ongoing training of all paid staff who supervise volunteers.

Training for paid staff can be an in-house program, or, in museums that do not have a training component in place, it can be provided by outside organizations. Staff training can be conducted as a one- to two-day concentrated program or scheduled in a number of sessions over a longer period. The topics must be sequenced properly, and the overall program must be comprehensive. Ongoing mini-sessions on current volunteer management topics can be held as the need arises. Like the training program for volunteers described in chapter 5, staff training should never become static but should continue to evolve along with the volunteer program.

A training curriculum for paid staff should include the following topics:

1. *An overview of voluntarism today.* Who are today's volunteers? What motivates them? What management techniques are most successful in working with them? A voluntary action center staff member can brief participants on the characteristics of the current volunteer pool in the community, including new types and sources of volunteers. Volunteers can also contribute their thoughts on the benefits of volunteering.

2. *The museum's current volunteer program.* The volunteer administrator or a volunteer organization leader should provide an overview of the program, followed by presentations from volunteers about their varied work in different parts of the museum.

3. *Recruitment and program planning.* In what projects—long-term or short-term—are volunteers needed? How will they be recruited? Participants should discuss setting goals for volunteer projects, developing the necessary assistance and training the department, and finding volunteers in the community to do the work. They should set a recruitment strategy and discuss frankly what volunteers can and cannot do in terms of their time and their other personal commitments.

4. *Management issues.* Participants should talk about such matters as organizational climate, management styles, the importance of two-way communication between volunteers and paid staff, and professional practices. Interactive techniques such as role-playing exercises and hypothetical problem-solving sessions can stimulate thought about management issues and provide practical suggestions for dealing with specific situations.

5. *Job descriptions for volunteers.* Participants should learn some guidelines for writing effective job descriptions and practice by writing hypothetical (or even actual) descriptions. Volunteers can be on hand to give feedback about job design. Since a good job description must provide measurable objec-

tives, this topic is closely related to the evaluation topic.

6. *Volunteer placement and training.* How is a volunteer matched with the appropriate job, and what types of training are necessary for different volunteer jobs in the museum? Participants should learn how to submit requests for volunteers and find out about the basics of placement and training as described in chapters 4 and 5.

7. *Evaluation and recognition.* Participants should discuss the purposes and techniques of performance evaluation for volunteers. A helpful exercise is role-playing an evaluation session involving a supervisor and a volunteer.

Volunteer leaders may collaborate in planning and conducting some of the training program sessions. For some sessions, however, it may be beneficial to have only staff attend to encourage them to communicate more openly among themselves. The decision will depend on the needs of the museum and current staff-volunteer relations. Once a core of staff supervisors has completed the training, communication should improve between staff and volunteers throughout the museum.

To enhance the value of the training, participants should be invited to assess the effectiveness of the program or materials. The assessment should take place about six months after the training, or after enough time has passed for supervisors to know whether and how the training helped them work with volunteers.

In addition to providing formal training, museums have found other ways of helping staff work more productively with volunteers. Paid staff can work periodically beside volunteers to review their performance in order to evaluate the success of their training. This technique also gives staff a way of experiencing the job from the volunteer's point of view. A sensitivity workshop for paid staff who work with volunteers can cover such topics as motivation, appropriate rewards, supervision, and schedules. Another way to orient staff is to encourage them to volunteer in other organizations. Those who have volunteered themselves have a clearer understanding of the volunteer's perspective.

Respecting Staff Expertise

Just as paid staff must understand and respect the motivations of volunteers and their potential for contributing to the museum, volunteers must value the expertise of staff members and respect the other demands of their jobs. Volunteer orientation and training programs should describe what staff members do. Often volunteers can learn about the work of the museum in general, and the staff members' roles in particular, through meetings in which staff talk about their jobs. Volunteers need to learn that time spent managing volunteer projects or consulting with volunteer leadership is only a small part of staff duties. They must respect the time demands on paid staff and allow staff the time they need to do their work. Volunteers must also respect a staff member's need for work areas that have limited access, even for other museum staff members.

Sometimes a volunteer program grows so large that it becomes necessary to hire paid staff for tasks that were originally done by volunteers. An example is a museum store operation that becomes too large and complex for a single volunteer manager to administer. The next step is often the hiring of a paid store manager. Volunteers should expect that this development will bring changes to their way of doing things. With increased volume and a salaried manager, changes in operation may be necessary. If volunteers have a stake in improving the museum store for the benefit of the museum, they may welcome the addition of a salaried manager. Open discussion in advance of how things will be different will help prepare volunteers for change.

Observing Professional Practices

As unpaid staff, volunteers must observe the same professional practices as the museum's paid staff. They must approach their responsibilities with the same commitment to professionalism as they would if they were compensated for their work. A statement of professional practices should describe the minimum standards to which a volunteer is expected to conform (see Figures 2.2, 2.3, 2.4). These standards usually govern everything from attendance to training to policies about resignation.

Volunteer leaders and staff supervisors should be trained and encouraged to deal with volunteers who do not adhere to these minimum standards, including unproductive volunteers and those who are troublesome to both staff and other volunteers. Ignoring problems will only exacerbate them, eventually morale will be damaged, and the positive relationships that have been established between staff and other volunteers will be affected. Facing any personnel problems head-on and professionally is the best course.

Trustees as Volunteers

In some museums, trustees may serve dual roles as board members and as volunteers. This is especially true for small or emerging museums in the early stages of institutional life (see chapter 2). In addition, many small historical museums have always operated as all-volunteer organizations, with trustees involved in governance, administration, and operations.

A trustee who is also a volunteer must take care to make a clear distinction between these two roles. As a board member, he or she has serious responsibilities related to the governance of the institution. These policy-making responsibilities are separate from the volunteer role.

When volunteers who also happen to be trustees lead a tour of the museum, work behind the scenes in a museum office, or greet visitors at the information desk, they function like any other volunteer under the direction of paid staff supervisors. They should not circumvent the authority of staff, nor should they expect special privileges because of their status as board members. Volunteers who work on board committees or associate with board members on social occasions should be aware of the lack of propriety in intermingling their social and volunteer roles. If trustees overstep their bounds as volunteers, it is up to the board chair to clarify to the individual board member what his or her proper role is in a volunteer position. In small museums with no paid staff, it may be difficult to maintain a clear distinction between trustee and volunteer functions, but the distinction is important nevertheless.

Mutual respect, a collegial atmosphere, a reciprocal appreciation for motivations, expertise, and interests—these are the basic ingredients of healthy communication between volunteers and paid staff. If there is a purposeful effort to forge and nurture good relations, everyone will benefit, and the museum's mission of public service will be invigorated.

7

TAKING STOCK

EVALUATING VOLUNTEERS AND THE VOLUNTEER PROGRAM

Evaluation is an invaluable element in the success and vitality of a museum volunteer program. Too often, the effectiveness of the program and the individual volunteers is measured in hours worked and money saved. But regular evaluation is a more appropriate measuring device with many benefits. For individual volunteers, a performance review is a positive opportunity. The constructive feedback a volunteer receives stimulates learning and improvement, recognizes achievement, and enhances both the volunteer's experience and the museum's public service. For the volunteer program, evaluation is an assessment and planning tool. If the program is meeting its goals and expectations, evaluation documents accomplishments and lays the foundation for continuing success. If the quality of the program falls short of its goals, evaluation highlights problem areas and supplies a starting point for instituting change.

Evaluating the Volunteer

Volunteers should understand when they are recruited and placed that they will undergo periodic performance reviews. No one eagerly anticipates having his or her job performance assessed, but it is a fact of professional life. Done appropriately, performance review can be a positive experience. To smooth the process, evaluation of the individual volunteer should begin with an annual self-evaluation process that encourages the volunteer to assess his or her own accomplishments and provide feedback about the volunteer experience. Self-evaluation eases the transition to the second component, an annual individual evaluation session with the volunteer's supervisor. The third component of individual evaluation is ongoing informal review consisting of praise and appreciation for a job well done and constructive suggestions for improvement.

Well-written volunteer job descriptions and a clear, specific volunteer agreement are the basis for evaluating the contributions of volunteers and the significant work they do for the museum. The descriptions and agreement should focus on specific responsibilities and measurable objectives so that volunteers, the volunteer administrator, and staff supervisors all have a clear understanding of expectations and obligations.

Self-Evaluation

A self-evaluation process encourages volunteers to assess their own accomplishments, reflect on aspects of their performance that they would like to improve, and think about how their jobs fulfill their expectations. Self-evaluation stimulates candor and careful thought by volunteers and is the stepping-stone to the formal performance review. Excellent ideas for enhancing or improving the volunteer program can also emerge from the self-evaluation process.

A self-evaluation form enables volunteers to assess their own performance and consider ways they might like to expand their volunteer involvement (see Figure 7-1). The job description and volunteer agreement may be attached to the blank form so the volunteer will have evaluation criteria readily available.

Individual Evaluation

A well-thought-out individual evaluation session is helpful both to the volunteer and the museum. The session should be designed to let the volunteer know that his or her work is valuable to the museum and that the program welcomes suggestions for improvement or change. Most museums schedule annual sessions involving the volunteer, the staff supervisor, and the volunteer administrator or a volunteer organization officer. The session should focus on the following points:

♦ Discussion of the volunteer's accomplishments and suggestions for improvement

FIGURE 7.1

Volunteer Self-Evaluation

The Docent Council of the Oakland Museum Association uses this self-evaluation questionnaire.

1. Why am I a docent?

2. What are three ways I could improve my performance as a docent?

3. As an active/sustaining docent do I fulfill my commitment?

   a. Arrive on time and remain for my shift even if no tours are scheduled?

   b. Always get a substitute when needed and notify my supervisor?

   c. Practice tour and compare tour techniques with other docents, research for additional information, study and review my gallery?

   d. Attend at least five continuing education programs as required?

   If you would like to be a supervisor or serve on a committee, or if you have any suggestions for improvements and/or changes in the docent program, please see your department chairman.

   Source: Docent Council,
   Oakland Museum Association
   1000 Oak Street
   Oakland, CA 94607
   (415) 273-3515

♦ Discussion of future work the volunteer will do for the museum

♦ Constructive feedback from the volunteer to improve working conditions, supervision, training, or job content.

In addition to the volunteer self-evaluation form, an evaluation form completed by the staff supervisor is an important preliminary step (Figure 7-2). The volunteer should receive a copy of the supervisor's report, and the supervisor should receive a copy of the volunteer's self-evaluation.

An evaluation session should cover the following key questions:

1. Which tasks in the job description occupied most of your time this year?

2. Which tasks were done only rarely or not at all? Should they be eliminated from the job description?

3. Were tasks performed that are not listed? Should they be added to the job description?

4. How would you assess your performance of each task?

5. What might help you to improve your performance of these tasks?

6. How would you describe the supervision you received on this assignment?

7. How helpful was the training you received?

8. What suggestions do you have that might make the work area more productive?

9. Do you wish to continue in this assignment?

10. Is there anything else you would like to tell us?[1]

The session not only shows how the individual volunteer is getting along but may also uncover gaps in training or reveal problems in departments where volunteers are working. Sometimes the volunteer is the target of criticism when the real fault lies with ineffective supervision. Volunteers whose performance is not acceptable are sometimes mirroring their supervisors' attitudes. Poor supervision of volunteers should be addressed and corrected, not ignored. Likewise, those who work well with volunteers should be recognized when the yearly volunteer recognition event takes place.

In addition to regular evaluation sessions, evaluation is also a vital part of an exit interview for a volunteer. It can bring the museum's agreement with the volunteer to a satisfying end, leaving the volunteer feeling respected and appreciated. By taking the time to talk to a person who is leaving, the staff supervisor or volunteer administrator can ask for his or her thoughts and suggestions about the volunteer program and find out about problems with the museum, supervisors, or other volunteers. This information can be used in planning future recruitment and training programs.

Ongoing Evaluation

Throughout the year, volunteers need informal feedback about their performance, including praise for jobs well done and constructive criticism when improvement is necessary. The volunteer administrator and staff supervisor need feedback from volunteers, too, to prevent problems from developing and

to learn about particularly satisfying aspects of the volunteer experience. Ongoing evaluation is really just another way to describe open communication: between volunteer and supervisor, supervisor and volunteer, administrator and supervisor, and administrator and volunteer.

Dismissing a Volunteer

Careful screening and placement will prevent problems with difficult or unproductive volunteers, and regular evaluation will help find solutions before problems become serious. But it is sometimes necessary to dismiss a volunteer. It is a myth that volunteers cannot be terminated. The best volunteers respect structure, adhere to professional standards, and welcome evaluation of their work. Although some feel that dismissing a volunteer may risk negative consequences, the consequences are potentially much more damaging if an unproductive volunteer is permitted to continue. When the volunteer administrator avoids dismissing a person who is not producing or is disruptive to the program, others volunteers receive the message that any level of performance is acceptable. This situation diminishes the stature of the program in the eyes of paid staff, museum administration, and sometimes even the public.

Volunteers who are dismissed are subject to the same legal protection as paid staff. The decision to terminate a volunteer must be supported by a written

FIGURE

7.2

Staff Supervisor's Evaluation Form

Please complete and return to Volunteer Office

Name

Assignment

Season Worked

Dependability:	Always	Nearly Always	Seldom	Never
Reports for work on time				
If unable to report, calls in or recruits a substitute				
Dresses appropriately for position				
Relationship with others:				

Is courteous and respectful to: staff
                                                  visitors
                                                  other volunteers				

Cooperates with: staff other volunteers				
Shows enthusiasm for job performed				
Works in a businesslike, serious manner				
Skills and growth:				
Attends training sessions				
Assimilates and uses "on-the-job" training				
Follows directives well				
Shows initiative: —Performs work within job scope without being told —When needed, does individual study/research				

Comments:

Department

Evaluator's Signature   Date

Source: Mystic Seaport
Greenmanville Avenue
Mystic, CT 06355
(203) 572-0711

FIGURE
7.3

Evaluation of Volunteer Experience

_____
Name

_____
For which office did you volunteer?

_____
Who was your supervisor?

Describe your volunteer responsibilities:

_____

_____

_____
Start date   End date

Please ✓ your response to the following:
How would you rate supervision and support?

☐ Excellent   ☐ Good

☐ Adequate   ☐ Less than adequate

Comments:

_____

_____

How would you rate your training?

☐ Excellent   ☐ Good

☐ Adequate   ☐ Less than adequate

Comments:

_____

_____

How would you describe the work?

☐ Interesting and rewarding

☐ Tedious and routine, yet worthwhile

☐ Menial and boring, not worthwhile

☐ Not what was expected

Comments:

_____

_____

How would you rate your volunteer assignment as an educational experience?

☐ Excellent   ☐ Good

☐ Average   ☐ Poor

Comments:

_____

_____

Why are you leaving your volunteer position?

_____

_____

What suggestions can you offer for improving services to volunteers?

_____

_____

Would you like to discuss another volunteer assignment? ☐ Yes ☐ No

Comments:

_____

_____

_____
Signature   Date

Source: Visitor Information and
Associates' Reception Center
Smithsonian Institution
Washington, DC 20560
(202) 357-2700

job description and volunteer agreement, performance evaluation reports, and documentation to support the reasons for dismissal. An appeals process must be available to the volunteer.

Inactive Volunteers

Volunteer administrators are sometimes unsure how to handle the problem of having long-term volunteers who, despite years of excellent service, are no longer able to be active in the program. Many of them may be strong financial supporters of the museum. One positive alternative is to create life membership status in the volunteer organization and promote inactive volunteers to volunteer emeritus. Volunteers awarded such status can be honored at an annual meeting and continue to receive the volunteer newsletter and invitations to all events. They could also retain some or all of the privileges they had as active volunteers.

Evaluating the Volunteer Program

Periodic evaluation of the volunteer program is a healthy process of reflection, revitalization, and renewal. It enables volunteers to step back from their regular responsibilities and take a broad view of the program's effectiveness at helping the museum achieve its mission of public service. Program evaluation brings specific results, too, such as improved proce-

dures, expanded recruiting efforts, or more realistic goals. It is a critical part of ongoing long-range planning for the museum and the program.

The core of a program evaluation should be a self-study involving individual volunteers, volunteer organization leaders, and museum staff. Some programs contract with an evaluation consultant to facilitate the self-study and prepare a report. Often a committee of the volunteer organization conducts the evaluation.

Individual volunteers and staff supervisors should be invited to make substantive contributions to the evaluation process. A written evaluation form is a convenient way to gather information (Figure 7.3); it is useful to follow up especially thoughtful or provocative comments with personal conversations. The goal is to seek broad participation and encourage all who are involved in the volunteer program to feel that they have a stake in its success.

The mission, goals, and objectives of the volunteer program are the starting point for a program evaluation. The evaluation should assess not only whether, how, and how well goals and objectives were met, but whether they represent realistic expectations for the museum and the volunteer program. This means addressing the following points:

♦ the actual quantity and quality of the work done by volunteers in each category (interpretive programs, visitor services, behind-the-scenes, fund-raising and special events, and community relations)

♦ which activities are so vital that they deserve additional support and which should be discontinued for lack of need

♦ whether delivery of services in certain areas is poor or should be redefined

♦ whether the volunteer group reflects the demographic makeup of the community and how well recruitment efforts are working

♦ how well volunteers serve the needs of visitors, paid staff, and the volunteer program office

♦ how the museum as a whole benefits from volunteer involvement

Reliable information about the quality of programs can come from program records and reports. It can also be derived from evaluation of particular programs. A museum's education department, for example, may have the mechanism in place to evaluate the success of an interpretive program. Or the volunteer program may want to assess the effectiveness of its behind-the-scenes services. There are many resources on conducting evaluation in the museum setting (see Resource Guide).

Volunteer program evaluation can only have a substantive impact if volunteer leaders and museum administrators are committed to implementing changes based on the results. For this reason, evaluation should become a natural, institutionalized part of the volunteer program. If it is conducted as a matter of course, it will be not just an obligatory exercise, but a serious endeavor with positive consequences.

RESOURCE and NETWORKING GUIDE

The purpose of the Resource and Networking Guide is to provide the kind of information that any museum can use to enhance its volunteer program, and ultimately, all of its programs. A second goal is to make that information easy to obtain, by connecting the user to the expertise of museum colleagues.

The information in the guide is intended to be comprehensive, but specifically relevant to museums, and to be representative of the museum community in the United States. Effort has been made to include examples of volunteer activities in institutions of each geographic region, budget level, discipline and organizational type. The information was collected between 1990 and 1992 through surveys and interviews conducted by Joan Kuyper, AAMV Directors and members, and additional research by Kathleen Huftalen. Responses to questionnaires published in *AVISO,* the newsletter of the American Association of Museums, and direct solicitation of individual museums provided the bulk of the information and brought to light fresh new ideas and innovative programs.

Section I of the guide closely supports the handbook with resources useful for developing a museum volunteer program, its ongoing administration and management. This section first identifies Primary Resources. These are organizations and reference tools that should become familiar to all museum professionals because they support the broad range of museum operations, or are part of the established body of knowledge in the field of volunteerism. The organization of material in this section corresponds to chapter and subheadings as they are found in the text of the handbook. When information overlaps, references for related subheadings are combined, i.e. "Interviewing and Selecting Volunteers."

Section II contains information on the actual work that volunteers accomplish in museums. This section describes volunteer activities in interpretation, behind-the-scenes work, visitor services, fund raising, and community outreach programs. This section is intended to be not only informative, but also inspirational. It includes a sampling of some truly creative and adventurous museum projects with contact information that makes it easy to share ideas and expertise.

Within the guide information is arranged under three main categories:

Resource Organizations

Organizations that deal specifically with the subject matter under consideration, within or outside of the museum world.

Museums With Expertise

Listings and contact information for museums with applicable programs, policies, or activities.

Written and Recorded Resources

Current bibliographic information, including some references available in cassette form.

In a few subject areas, relevant information was found in only one or two of these categories.

A VITAL RESOURCE
Volunteers and Museums

PRIMARY RESOURCES

Resource Organizations

Museums should consider the following organizations first references in planning and administering volunteer programs. Each represents museums of all sizes and disciplines and addresses issues concerning volunteerism in the museum setting.

All hold annual conferences, intermittent educational programs, and special focus groups, and produce journals, newsletters and other technical assistance.

American Association of Museums
1225 Eye Street, NW
Washington, DC 20005
(202) 289-1818

Accredits museums and administers three Museum Assessment Programs. Public Dimension Assessment, MAP III, assists in many areas particularly relevant to volunteer service. Of eleven standing professional committees, Museum Education, Visitor Research and Evaluation, Exhibitions, Development and Membership, Public Relations, and Museum Professional Training address issues affecting volunteers. Technical Information Service can provide sample documents such as job descriptions, bylaws, and mission statements and can assist with referrals and networking.

American Association for
Museum Volunteers
c/o The American Association of Museums
1225 Eye Street, NW
Washington, DC 20005
(202) 289-6575

Represents more than 370,000 museum volunteers in all categories of museums. Members include museum volunteers, volunteer administrators, other staff members who work with volunteers, volunteer committees, and affiliates in the United States and Canada. Affiliated nationally with the American Association of Museums and internationally with the World Federation of Friends of Museums. Sponsors programs at national, regional, and local museum meetings. Quarterly newsletter.

Museum Trustees Association
1101 Connecticut Avenue, NW, Suite 700
Washington, DC 20036
(202) 857-1180

Organization of 158 member institutions serves volunteers concerned with policy issues, ethics, fund-raising, and administration. Quarterly newsletter, *Trusteeship*. Two annual conferences.

National Docent Symposium Council
High Museum of Art
1280 Peachtree Street, NE
Atlanta, GA 30309
(404) 898-9502

Holds biennial conference attended by 400 docents and staff delegates with sessions on such topics as docent enrichment, current issues, administration, and audience evaluation. Publications.

US Foundation for the World Federation of Friends of Museums
2 East Gittings Avenue
Baltimore, MD 21212
(301) 435-5791

Holds international conference of friends organizations and provides a worldwide link among these groups.

Regional Museum Associations

These associations provide a network for those involved in volunteer administration and every other aspect of museum operation. They promote partnership and sharing of resources and ideas, sponsor training opportunities such as seminars, and volunteer management roundtables and serve as clearinghouses for information of regional interest. Several have established databases on museum projects and programs.

New England Museum Association
Boston National Historical Park
Charleston Navy Yard
Boston, MA 02129
(617) 720-1573

For Connecticut, Maine, Massachusetts, New Hampshire, Rhode Island, and Vermont.

Mid-Atlantic Association of Museums
P.O. Box 817
Newark, DE 19711
(302) 731-1424

For Delaware, District of Columbia, Maryland, New Jersey, New York, and Pennsyvania.

Midwest Museum Conference
P.O. Box 11940
St. Louis, MO 63112
(314) 454-3110

For Illinois, Indiana, Iowa, Michigan, Minnesota, Missouri, Ohio, and Wisconsin.

Southeastern Museums Conference
P.O. Box 3494
Baton Rouge, LA 70821
(504) 343-4341

For Alabama, Arkansas, Florida, Georgia, Kentucky, Louisiana, Mississippi, North Carolina, South Carolina, Tennessee, Virginia, and West Virginia.

Mountain-Plains Museum Association
Pro Rodeo Association
P.O. Box 335
Manitou Springs, CO 80829
(719) 593-8840

For Colorado, Kansas, Montana, Nebraska, New Mexico, North Dakota, Oklahoma, South Dakota, Texas and Wyoming.

Western Museums Conference
700 State Drive, Room 130
Los Angeles, CA 90037
(213) 749-0119

For Alaska, Arizona, California, Hawaii, Idaho, Nevada, Oregon, Utah, and Washington.

State Museum Associations

Approximately forty-five state museum associations support museums of every discipline on the local level. Many have field service representatives who will visit an institution for individual consultations or to hold training programs. Contact your regional museum association for more information on statewide organizations.

Discipline-Related Resource Organizations

American Association
for State and Local History
172 Second Avenue North, Suite 202
Nashville, TN 37201
(615) 255-2971

American Association of
Botanical Gardens and Arboreta
786 Church Road
Wayne, PA 19087
(215) 688-1120

American Association of
Zoological Parks and Aquariums
Ogelby Park, Route 88
Wheeling, WV 26003
(304) 242-2160

American Council for the Arts
One East 53rd Street
New York, NY 10022
(212) 223-2787

American Federation of Arts
41 East 65th Street
New York, NY 10021
(212) 988-7700

Association of College and
University Museums
University Museum
Southern Illinois University
Edwardsville, IL 62026-1150
(618) 692-2996

Association of Science-Technology Centers
1413 K Street, NW
Washington, DC 20005
(202) 371-1171

Association of Youth Museums
Staten Island Children's Museum
1000 Richmond Terrace
Staten Island, NY 10301
(718) 273-2493

National Endowment for the Arts
1100 Pennsylvania Avenue, NW
Washington, DC 20506
(202) 682-5442

National Endowment for the Humanities
1100 Pennsylvania Avenue, NW
Washington, DC 20506
(202) 606-8284

National Trust for Historic Preservation
1785 Massachusetts Avenue, NW
Washington, DC 20036
(202) 673-4000

Volunteer Committees of Art Museums
Philbrook Museum of Art
2727 South Rockford Road
Tulsa, OK 74114
(918) 749-5279

General References on Volunteer Administration

ACTION
1100 Vermont Avenue, NW
Washington, DC 20525
(202) 606-4806
    This federal domestic volunteer agency is the umbrella organization for many programs including the Retired Senior Volunteer Program (RSVP) and the Student Community Service Program. Regional offices in Boston, New York, Atlanta, Philadelphia, Dallas, Denver. Consult the government section of your telephone directory for local contact.

Association for Volunteer Administration
P.O. Box 4584
Boulder, CO 80306
(303) 497-0238

Sponsors regional CVA (Certified in Volunteer Administration) qualification. Publishes the *Journal of Volunteer Administration* and other technical information. Annual meeting.

Independent Sector
1828 L Street, NW
Washington, DC 20036
(202) 223-8100

Advocacy group serves membership of major health, social services, arts, and other nonprofits, foundations and other voluntary organizations. Sponsors studies on giving and volunteering, publishes data and book series on volunteer subjects from board administration to management materials.

National VOLUNTEER Center/
Points of Light Foundation
736 Jackson Place, NW
Washington, DC 20503
(202) 408-5162

Publishes *Voluntary Action Leadership,* which contains articles on management issues, lists of current publications in the field, writings of national leaders in volunteer management, and reports on changes in the law in the area of liability, and taxes.

Other Organizations

Most states now have offices of volunteerism which actively sponsor conferences, provide networking and volunteering information. Such services may be found by contacting your State Office of Volunteerism, the National Governors' Association, the National Council of State Governments or Voluntary Action Centers

Regional, county or city centers that serve as clearinghouses for volunteer placement and information. Many conduct sessions on volunteer orientation, training, and management.

Publishers

These publishers specialize in business, management, and volunteer information.

Augsburg Publishing House
Box 1209
Minneapolis, MN 55440
(800) 329-4648

Energize, Inc.
5450 Wissihickon Avenue, Lobby A
Philadelphia, PA 19144
(215) 438-8342

Heritage Arts Publishing
1807 Prairie Avenue
Downers Grove, IL 60515
(312) 964-1194

Jossey-Bass Inc.
350 Sansome Street
San Francisco, CA 94104
(415) 433-1767

Mcduff/Blunt Associates
821 Lincoln Street
Walla Walla, WA 99362
(509) 529-0244

Marlborough Publications
P.O. Box 16406
San Diego, CA 92116

Public Management Institute
358 Brennan Street
San Francisco, CA 94107

Society for Nonprofit Organizations
6314 Odana Road, Suite 1
Madison, WI 53719
(608) 274-9777

Taft Group
5130 MacArthur Boulevard, NW
Washington, DC 20016
(800) 424-3761

Vancouver Volunteer Centre
1625 West 8th Avenue
Vancouver, BC V6J -1T9
(604) 731-6168

Voluntary Management Press, Inc.
P.O. Box 9170
Downers Grove, IL 60515

Volunteer Management Associates
1113 Spruce Street, Suite 406-A
Boulder, CO 80302-4049
(303) 447-0558

Written and Recorded Resources

Brainerd, Susan, and Joan Kuyper, eds. "Volunteerism in the Arts." *Journal of Arts Management and Law* 17 (Summer 1987).

Articles on the history of arts volunteering, museum volunteering, trusteeship,and model programs. Also features a roundtable discussion on cultural volunteering.

Burcaw, G. Ellis. *Introduction to Museum Work.* Nashville, TN: American Association for State and Local History, 1975.

Butcher-Younghans, Sherry. "Using Volunteers in History." *History News* 43 (July/August 1988): 11-14.

Chadwick, Alan, and Eilean Hooper-Greenhill. "Volunteers in Museums and Galleries: A Discussion of Some of the Issues." *Museums Journal* 84 (March 1984): 177.

Chapin, Isolde, and Richard Mock. *New Faces in Public Places: Volunteers in the Humanities.* Washington, DC: Volunteer Readership of the Points of Light Foundation, 1979.

Cloutier, Anne. "Volunteers Unlimited." *Nature Study* 36 (March 1983): 14-15.

Opportunities for docents in zoos, museums, art galleries, and nature centers.

Excellence and Equity: Education and the Public Dimension of Museums. Washington, DC: American Association of Museums, 1991.

Kopper, Philip. *Volunteer! O Volunteer! A Salute to the Smithsonian's Unpaid Legions.* Washington, DC: Smithsonian Institution Press, (undated).

Accomplishments and contributions of Smithsonian volunteers.

Moses, Barbara S. *Volunteers in Zoos and Aquariums: A Resource Manual.* Wheeling, WV: American Association of Zoological Parks and Aquariums, 1981.

Nicholson, Thomas D. "Volunteer Employment in the American Museum of Natural History." *Curator* 26 (September 1983): 241-53.

Nielsen, Marian. *A Directory of Museum Volunteer Programs.* Washington, DC: American Association for Museum Volunteers, 1988.

Wide variety of volunteer activities in 700 museum, with specific contact information.

CHAPTER 2

Laying the Groundwork

The Volunteer Program's Mission and Structure

DEVELOPING A LONG-RANGE PLAN: BUILDING ORGANIZATIONAL SUPPORT

Resource Organizations

American Association of Museums
1225 Eye Street, NW
Washington, DC 20005
(202) 289-1818

Has several publications on institutional planning, listed below. Technical Information Service will furnish members samples of bylaws, mission statements, professional practices and standards statements and other organizational tools designed specifically for museum volunteers.

Regional Museum Associations

Good source for referrals, matching similar situations, disseminating successful approaches to solving common situations. Invaluable base for networking, especially for the smaller institution.

Museums With Expertise

All of the following museums have well-defined written organizational tools. This list is a sampling of institutions of varying disciplines, budgets, and geographical locations.

Complete organizational documents are required for accreditation by the American Association of Museums, so many accredited museums could serve as equally valuable models. Consult *Official Museum Directory* for the names of more accredited museums.

Brattleboro Museum and Art Center
Main & Vermont Streets
P.O. Box 662
Brattleboro, VT 05302
(802) 257-0124

Well developed mission statement, also "Rights of Volunteers/Responsibilities of Volunteers."

Cumberland Science Museum
800 Ridley Boulevard
Nashville, TN 37203
(615) 259-6099

Mission statement, volunteer program goals, guidelines.

Detroit Institute of Art Founders Society
5200 Woodward Avenue
Detroit, MI 48202
(313) 833-7900

Founders Society has many auxiliary support groups including a women's and a volunteer committee, committees supporting a number of galleries, and a trip program. Well-structured bylaws and policies for the organization, professional practices for the volunteer program that apply to both paid staff and volunteers.

Kansas State Historical Society
Kansas Museum of History
6425 SW Sixth
Topeka, KS 66615-1099
(913) 272-8761

Volunteer organization has policy statement for volunteers, docent guidelines.

Magnolia Mound Plantation
2161 Nicholson Drive
Baton Rouge, LA 70802
(504) 343-4955
Mound Builders Volunteer Handbook includes statement of purpose, museum ethics for volunteers.

North Carolina Museum of Art
2110 Blue Ridge Boulevard
Raleigh, NC 27607
(919) 833-1935
Well written mission statement, written in 1989.

Written and Recorded Sources

Barry, Bryan W. *Strategic Planning Workbook for Nonprofit Organizations.* Amherst H. Wilder Foundation, 1986.
Step-by-step guide to planning. Includes examples and worksheets.

Ellis, Susan J., John Paul Dalsimer, and Jeffrey D. Kahn. *From the Top Down: The Executive Role in Volunteer Program Success.* Philadelphia: Energize Associates, 1986.

Flanagan, Joan. *The Successful Volunteer Organization: Getting Started and Getting Results in Nonprofit, Charitable, Grass Roots and Community Groups.* Chicago: Contemporary Books, Inc., 1984.

Fletcher, Kathleen Brown. *The 9 Keys to Successful Volunteer Programs.* Washington DC: Taft Group, 1987.

George, Gerald, and Cindy Sherrell-Leo. *Starting Right, A Basic Guide to Museum Planning.* Nashville, TN: AASLH Press, 1987.
Institutional long-range planning information readily applicable to volunteer program planning.

Hardy, James M. *Managing for Impact in Nonprofit Organizations: Corporate Planning Techniques and Applications.* Erwin, TX: Essex Press, 1984.

Karn, Neil. "The No-Apologies Budget." *Voluntary Action Leadership* (Spring 1984): 29-31.

McBride, Marie, and Joan Kuyper. "Arts and Humanities: Volunteers are the Answer." *Voluntary Action Leadership* (Spring 1981): 16-17.
A training program for organizations on volunteer administration.

Nichols, Susan K., ed. *Organizing Your Museum: The Essentials.* Washington, DC: American Association of Museums Technical Information Service, 1989.
Includes articles on long-range planning, position descriptions, mission statements and policies, all easily applied to volunteer programs.

Shaping the Museum: The MAP Institutional Planning Guide. Washington, DC: American Association of Museums, 1990.
Institutional long-range planning information readily applicable to volunteer program planning.

Sullivan, Patricia. "Volunteers: How to Build a Strong Support Staff for Your Institution." *History News* 37 (October 1982): 19-21.

UNDERSTANDING LEGAL AND ETHICAL REQUIREMENTS

Resource Organizations

American Law Institute (ALI)
4025 Chestnut Street
Philadelphia, PA 19104-3099
(215) 243-1600

Together with the American Bar Association, ALI holds annual conference, "Legal Problems of Museum Administration," for museum professionals and produces an annual publication of the same name.

Volunteers Insurance Service
Corporate Management Inc.
216 South Peyton Street
Alexandria, VA 22314
(800) 468-4200

San Antonio Museums Association
200 West Jones Avenue
San Antonio, TX 78215
(512) 978-8100

Published guidelines to define limits within museum/support group relationship.

Museums With Expertise

Indianapolis Zoo
1200 West Washington Street
Indianapolis, IN 46218
(317) 638-8072

Volunteer handbook includes a comprehensive ethics statement.

Pacific Science Center
200 Second Avenue North
Seattle, WA 98109
(206) 443-2001

This museum's volunteer program documents include a volunteer disclosure statement that is a legal requirement of the state of Washington.

Written and Recorded Resources

Code of Ethics for Museums. Washington, DC: American Association of Museums, 1991.

Chapman, Terry S., Mary L. Lai, and Elmer L. Steinbock, *Am I Covered . . . ? A Guide to Insurance for Nonprofit Organizations.* San Jose, CA: Consortium for Human Services, 1984.

Guidance about liability issues, property and volunteer insurance, worker's compensation.

ICOM Statutes and Code of Professional Ethics. Paris: International Council of Museums, 1990.

Nielsen, Marian. "Ethics Codes and Museum Volunteers." *The Public Garden* 6 (October 1991): 17.

Professional Codes of Ethics: Museum News Reprint Package. Washington, DC: American Association of Museums, 1989.

Includes codes of ethics for curators, conservators, registrars, museum stores personnel, and educators, along with selected readings.

Selby, Robert T. "Bylaws for Volunteer Groups." *Museum News* 56 (September/October 1977): 24-26.

Singer, Gerald R. "Make Sure Support Groups *Support* You, Not *Undermine* You." *Museum News* 69 (July/Aug 1990): 31-33.

Writing a Museum Code of Ethics. Washington, DC: American Association of Museums Technical Information Service, 1992.

A guide for developing an institutional code of ethics. Includes sample codes, case studies, and discussion of "What Is Ethics?"

ESTABLISHING A PROGRAM STRUCTURE

Museums With Expertise

The museums listed include both integrated and independent organizational structures.

Birmingham Botanical Gardens
2612 Lane Park Road
Birmingham, AL 35223
(205) 879-1227
Birmingham Botanical Society is the primary fund-raising and support group for the gardens. 1500 member group arranges educational activities, special events, helps guide garden's development, leads free educational class each Sunday.

Carnegie Institute
4400 Forbes Avenue
Pittsburg, PA 15215
(412) 622-3243
Volunteer program under paid coordinator, also two ancillary support groups: Women's Committee, Museum of Art; and Council for Carnegie Museum of Natural History.

Detroit Institute of Art Founders Society
5200 Woodward Avenue
Detroit, MI 48202
(313) 833-7900
Founders Society has many auxiliary support groups including a women's and a volunteer committee, committees supporting a number of galleries, and a trip program. Well-structured bylaws and policies for the organization, professional practices for the volunteer program for both paid staff and volunteers.

Hagley Museum and Library
P.O. Box 3630
Wilmington, DE 19807
(302) 658-2400
Integrated volunteer program with paid administrator.

Lexington Historical Society
P.O. Box 514
Lexington, MA 02173
(617) 862-1703
Hundred-year old all-volunteer society hired its first professional director in 1992.

Los Angeles County Museum of Art
5905 Wilshire Boulevard
Los Angeles, CA 90036
(213) 857-6111
Large complex independent structure.

Museum of History & Science
727 North Main Street
Louisville, KY 40202-2681
Plans to incorporate more structure into volunteer program.

Museum of Science & Industry
57th and Lake Shore Drive
Chicago, IL 60637-2093
(312) 684-1414
Anticipates positive change for volunteer program from recent shift in administration from education department to development/membership.

Renwick Gallery of the National Museum of American Art
The Smithsonian Institution
Pennsylvania Avenue & 17th Street, NW
Washington, DC 20560
(202) 357-2700
Has excellent example of docent bylaws, written in 1987.

New York Zoological Society
185th Street & Southern Boulevard
Bronx, NY 10460
(212) 220-5141
Integrated volunteer program with paid administrator.

Wadsworth Athenaeum
600 Main Street
Hartford, CT 06103
(203) 278-2670

Independent support organization with comprehensive "Bylaws for Volunteer and Affiliated Organizations," with a well developed description of the relationship between the organization and the museum.

Written and Recorded Resources

Macduff, Nancy. *Building Effective Volunteer Committees.* Walla Walla, WA: Macduff/Bunt Associates, 1986.

Muench, Elizabeth N. "Volunteer Programs Run by Volunteers: The Women's Committee of the Wadsworth Atheneum." *American Association for Museum Volunteers Newsletter* (Spring) 1990, 2.

Rauner, Judy. *Helping People Volunteer.* San Diego: Marlborough Publications, 1980.

Program design workbook with twenty worksheets to evaluate existing program and guide growth of volunteer program.

CHAPTER 3

Options for Leadership
Program Administration

RESPONSIBILITIES AND QUALIFICATIONS OF THE VOLUNTEER ADMINISTRATOR

Written and Recorded Resources

Brown, Winifred L. "The Role of the Volunteer Administrator." *Association for Volunteer Administration Update* (July/August 1988): 3-4.

Cox, Ted. *Volunteer Program Management Guide: A Practical Manual for Planning and Managing a Science Center Volunteer Program.* Washington, DC: Association of Science Technology Centers, 1989.

Ellis, Susan J., and Katherine H. Noyes. *No Excuses: The Team Approach to Volunteer Management.* Philadelphia: Energize, Inc., 1981.

For organizations without a full-time volunteer coordinator.

Kessler, Patricia Powell, and Ruth Ann O'Connell, eds. "Museum Volunteers: Management, Resources and Case Studies." *Journal of Museum Education* 11 (Summer 1986): entire issue.

Management of Museum Volunteers. Washington, DC: Smithsonian Institution Visitor Information and Associates Reception Center, 1987.

Informative eleven-page brochure maps out the essentials.

McConkey, Lois. *From Boredom to Burnout: A Manual on Volunteerism.* Vancouver: University of British Columbia Museum of Anthropology, 1985.

McCurley, Steve. *Volunteer Management Policies.* Downers Grove, IL: Heritage Arts Publishing, 1990.

McCurley, Stephen, and Sue Vineyard. *101 Ideas for Volunteer Programs.* Downers Grove, IL: Heritage Arts Publishing, 1986.

Seita, Trudy, and Sue Waechter. *Change: How to Meet It and Greet It.* Downers Grove, IL: Heritage Arts Publishing, 1991.

Wilson, Marlene. *The Effective Management of Volunteer Programs.* Boulder, CO: Volunteer Management Associates, 1976.

The "bible" for volunteer administrators. Current management theories on leadership, motivation, planning, and evaluation.

PROFESSIONAL DEVELOPMENT FOR VOLUNTEER MANAGERS

Resource Organizations

Standing Professional Committee on Museum Professional Training of the American Association of Museums c/o American Association of Museums 1225 Eye Street, NW Washington, DC 20005 (202) 289-1818

Regional Volunteer Managers Roundtables
Often loosely structured, roundtable groups are providing new networking opportunities for volunteer managers and program administrators on volunteerism in cultural institutions.
Contact regional museums associations for information on local roundtables.

New England Volunteer Managers Roundtable
Society for the Preservation of New England Antiquities
141 Cambridge
Boston, MA 02114
(617) 227-3956
A professional affinity group of the New England Museums Association which meets four times a year, holds day-long symposiums, and is currently working on a handbook on volunteer program management.

Oahu Museum Volunteer Leaders
Bishop Museum
P.O. Box 19000-A
Honolulu, HI 96817-0916
(808) 847-3511
Conducts joint training and brainstorming sessions for art, history, and natural science museum volunteers.

Volunteer Program Administrators in Cultural Institutions
Horticulture Society of New York
128 West 58th Street
New York, NY 10019
(212) 757-0915
Five-year-old organization of 128 members meets monthly to discuss such topics as recruitment, training, and evaluation.

Written and Recorded Resources

DeCarlo, Mary. "Performance-Based Certification—An Avenue for Professional Development and Recognition." *Voluntary Action Leadership* (Fall 1983): 25-27.

Morrison, Emily Kittle. *Skills for Leadership: Working With Volunteers.* Tucson, AZ: Jordan Press, 1983.

Webb, Jody. "A Profile of Volunteer Management Education." Boulder, CO: Association for Volunteer Administration, 1992.
Includes a list of colleges and universities offering volunteer management education in the United States and Canada.

DESIGNING VOLUNTEER JOBS: JOB DESCRIPTIONS

Museums With Expertise

These museums have well-designed volunteer jobs and examples of job descriptions for museum guides, visitor information volunteers, collections assistants, clerical and museum shop volunteers, and other institution-specific volunteer positions, such as honorary curator and "back-in-time" volunteer.

The Depot
St. Louis County Heritage and Arts Center
506 West Michigan Street
Duluth, MN 55802
(218) 727-8025

Field Museum of Natural History
Roosevelt Road at Lake Shore Drive
Chicago, IL 60605-2496
(312) 922-9410

Historic Annapolis Foundation
194 Prince Georges Street
Annapolis, MD 21401
(301) 267-8149

Renwick Gallery of the National
Museum of American Art
The Smithsonian Institution
Pennsylvania Avenue & 17th Street, NW
Washington, DC 20560
(202) 357-2700

St. Louis Science Center
5050 Oakland Avenue
St. Louis, MO 63110
(314) 289-4400

Virginia Living Museum
524 J. Clyde Morris Boulevard
Newport News, VA 23601
(804) 595-1900

Written and Recorded Resources

Meltzer, Phyllis J. "Help Them Help You." *Museum News* 67 (March/April 1988): 60-62.
Negotiated volunteer service agreement.

Wallace, Patricia. "Volunteers Can Meet Professional Standards." *History News* 35 (June 1980): 8-9.

VOLUNTEER SUPERVISION

Written and Recorded Resources

Brown, Kathleen M. "Thoughts on the Supervision of Volunteers." *Voluntary Action Leadership* (Spring 1984): 14-16.
Supervising volunteers is not the same as supervising paid staff and the differences are important.

Moore, Larry F. *Motivating Volunteers: How the Rewards of Unpaid Work Can Meet People's Needs.* Vancouver, Canada: Vancouver Volunteer Center, 1985.
Essays on job design, goal setting, and needs profiles, with many examples in a museum context.

Skillingstad, Connie. "Training Supervisors of Volunteers." *Journal of Volunteer Administration* 8 (Winter 1989-90): 29-32.

MAINTAINING VOLUNTEER RECORDS AND REPORTS

Individual manual record-keeping systems are in wide use, but many museums are now incorporating a variety of off-the-shelf software, or custom programs to track volunteer data. Only a few are listed here; regional museum associations can help locate good models in comparable institutions.

Museums with Expertise

Portland Art Museum
1219 SW Park Avenue
Portland, OR 97205
(503) 226-2811
Database system for record keeping.

Santa Cruz Museum Association
1305 East Cliff Drive
Santa Cruz, CA 95062
(408) 429-3773

Uses Versaform, a PC-compatible computer system to track volunteer information.

Smithsonian Institution
Visitor Information and Associates
Reception Center
Washington, DC 20560
(202) 357-2700

Uses Matchpoint, a commercially available software package to track volunteer information.

Written and Recorded Resources

Ellis, Susan J., and Katherine H. Noyes. *Proof Positive: Developing Significant Volunteer Recordkeeping Systems.* Philadelphia: Energize, Inc., 1981.

The Volunteer Management System (VMS). Q.L. Software, Inc. Computer-assisted program with ability to maintain personnel profiles, keep activity history, record hours and awards, produce newsletter and annual report.

CHAPTER 4

Cultivating Volunteer Interest
Recruitment and Selection

DEVELOPING RECRUITMENT GOALS

Museums With Expertise

State Historical Society of North Dakota
North Dakota Heritage Center
Capitol Grounds
Bismarck, ND 58505
(701) 224-2674
Has well-developed recruitment goals and tools: job descriptions, newsletters, brochures.

Jewish Museum
1109 Fifth Avenue
New York, NY 10128
(212) 860-1888
In 1988 began a marketing approach to recruitment to make efficient use of limited staff resources.

Pacific Science Center
200 Second Avenue North
Seattle, WA 98109
(206) 443-2001
Written recruitment plan and goals.

Whitney Museum of American Art
945 Madison Avenue
New York, NY 10021
(212) 570-3600
Plan focuses on recruiting volunteers from colleges.

Written and Recorded Resources

Lynch, Richard. "Preparing an Effective Recruitment Campaign." *Voluntary Action Leadership* (Winter 1984): 23-27.

Macduff, Nancy. *Volunteer Recruiting and Retention: A Marketing Approach.* Walla Walla, WA: Macduff/Bunt Associates, 1983.

Vineyard, Sue, and Steve McCurley. *101 Tips for Volunteer Recruitment.* Downers Grove, IL: Heritage Arts Publishing, 1988.

Wilson, Marlene. *Recruiting and Interviewing Volunteers.* Boulder, CO: Volunteer Management Associates, 1992.
Audio or videocassette.

SOURCES OF VOLUNTEERS

WORKING PEOPLE

Resource Organizations

Arts and Business Council, Inc.
25 West 45th Street
New York, NY 10036
(212) 819-9287
Business Volunteers for the Arts is a partnership program between the arts community and business that recruits, orients, and places business executives as management consultants with nonprofit arts organizations on a volunteer basis. Affiliates operate in thirty cities under the auspices of BVA/USA, its national program.

Business Committee for the Arts
1775 Broadway
New York, NY 10019
(212) 664-0600

Encourages business to support arts organizations with money, volunteer assistance, donated services and products, joint marketing, advertising, and promotional efforts.

Museums With Expertise

Chicago Architecture Foundation
1800 South Prairie Avenue
Chicago, IL 60616
(312) 326-1393

Of a volunteer force of 275, 65 percent work weekends and evenings and 30 percent are men.

Conner Prairie
13400 Allisonville Road
Noblesville, IN 46060-4499
(317) 776-6000

Corporate volunteers staff seasonal special events.

Denver Museum of Natural History
City Park
Denver, CO 80205
(303) 370-6420

Weekend volunteer programs, including interpreters and demonstrators.

Los Angeles County Museum of Art
5905 Wilshire Boulevard
Los Angeles, CA 90036
(213) 857-6111

Art Membership Renewal Committee. Volunteers work evenings and weekends calling other members to renew.

Studio Museum in Harlem
144 West 125th Street
New York, NY 10027
(212) 864-4500

Extensive program utilizing business volunteers and retired teachers.

Tampa Museum of Art
Friends of the Arts
601 Doyle Carlton Drive
Tampa, FL 33602
(813) 223-8130

A business volunteer group of career men and women.

Toledo Museum of Art
2445 Monroe Street
Toledo, OH 43620
(419) 255-8000

Conducted a pilot program for recruiting volunteers from the professional work force.

Phoenix Art Museum
1625 North Central
Phoenix, AZ 85004
(602) 257-1880

Has active Men's Council.

Written and Recorded Resources

Nickerson, Ann T. "How to Set up a Corporate Volunteer Program." *History News* (September 1983): 34-37.

Stellwagen, A. *Recruiting and Training Working People and Minorities as Docents: A Report, Evaluation, and Recommendations on a Pilot Project at the Toledo Museum of Art.* Toledo, OH: Toledo Museum of Art, October 1987.

Vizza, Cynthia, Kenn Allen and Shirley Keller. *A New Competitive Edge: Volunteers from the Workplace.* Washington, DC: Volunteer Readership of the Points of Light Foundation, 1986.

RETIRED PEOPLE

Resource Organizations

American Association of Retired Persons
Office of Volunteer Coordination
601 E Street, NW
Washington, DC 20049
(202) 434-2277

Volunteer skills bank of retired professionals and volunteers in museum programs.

National Executive Service Corps
257 Park Avenue South
New York, NY
(212) 529-6660

Volunteer retired company presidents and top executives serve as consultants to nonprofits in areas such as strategic planning, computerization, fiscal management, and marketing, for a small fee.

Retired Senior Volunteer Program
1100 Vermont Avenue
Washington, DC 20525
(202) 606-4853

RSVP, a program of ACTION, the Federal Domestic Volunteer Program has offices in major American cities. Thousands of seniors volunteer through the program as weekly staff support, for special events, and on skilled and professional projects. Consult federal government listing of local telephone directory.

Museums With Expertise

Boston Museum of Fine Arts
Looking Together Program
Outreach to Senior Citizens
465 Huntington Avenue
Boston, MA 02115
(617) 267-9300

A program of off-site volunteering involving older adults in the Boston area. Training program for twenty older volunteers and an outreach program to reach 400 seniors in nursing homes and senior centers.

Capitol Children's Museum
800 Third Street, NE
Washington, DC 20002
(202) 675-4127

Ten-year-old senior volunteer program has adapted to changes in economy, and in program goals. Seniors conduct exhibition activities, and work behind-the-scenes. Small stipend for volunteers through RSVP grant.

Santa Cruz Museum Association
1305 East Cliff Drive
Santa Cruz, CA 95062
(408) 429-3773

Seniors do frequent short tasks, such as helping with membership mailings.

YOUNG PEOPLE

Resource Organizations

Association of Youth Museums
Staten Island Children's Museum
1000 Richmond Terrace
Staten Island, NY 10301
(718) 273-2493

Student Community Service Project
ACTION
1100 Vermont Avenue
Washington, DC 20525
(202) 606-4824

A program of ACTION, the Federal Domestic Volunteer Agency. Local offices throughout the United States help direct young people to worthwhile volunteer activities.

Museums With Expertise

Austin Children's Museum
1501-A West Fifth Street
Austin, TX 78703
(512) 472-2494

Continual evolution of youth program begun in 1987. Conducted internal program evaluation in 1989, and a field survey of youth volunteer programs in science and youth museums, which resulted in the publication *Youth Volunteer Programs in Museums*, listed below.

Cabrillo Marine Museum
3720 Stephen White Drive
San Pedro, CA 90731
(213) 548-7562

Summer program for junior high and high school students. One week training, one morning per week service reqirement. $50 cost.

Historical Society of York County
250 East Market Street
York, PA 17403
(717) 848-1587

Junior docents must have completed eighth grade and be recommended by social studies teachers. Duties include guiding tours at historic houses, assisting with admissions, and working in museum shop as needed.

Lakeview Museum of Arts & Sciences
1125 West Lake Avenue
Peoria, IL 61614-5985
(309) 686-7000

Summer junior-volunteer program for graduating eighth graders through high school. Emphasizes learning through public service.

South Street Seaport Museum
207 Front Street
New York, NY 10038
(212) 669-9400

High school volunteers crew, do maintenance and carpentry on historic ships, do clerical work and data entry, and work in collections, education, and the museum shop.

Virginia Living Museum
524 J. Clyde Morris Boulevard
Newport News, VA 23601
(804) 595-1900

Junior curator program for ages fourteen through seventeen.

Written and Recorded Sources

Edward, Deborah, Chan McDermott, and Sarita Rodriguez. *Youth Volunteer Programs in Museums.* Austin, TX: Austin Children's Museum, 1989.

A study of youth volunteer programs in 200 museums. Participation by the Association of Youth Museums and the Association of Science-Technology Centers. Funded by Lily Endowment.

Ellis, Susan J., with Katherine H. Noyes, Trina Tracy and Lawrence Wallace. *Children as Volunteers.* Philadelphia: Energize, Inc., 1991.

Nickerson, Ann T. "Is It Fun? Is It History? A Teen-age Volunteer Corps Learns History and Lightens the Workload at Old Economy Village." *History News* 38 (September 1985): 30-33.

SOURCES OF VOLUNTEERS

UNDERGRADUATE AND GRADUATE INTERNSHIPS

Resource Organizations

The following colleges and universities have programs that provide business and management students as consultants to nonprofit organizations. Colleges and universities can also give guidance if setting up a new program.

University of Chicago (312) 996-2285

Boston College (617) 552-3161

Carnegie-Mellon University (412) 268-2166

Stanford University, Business Development Association (415) 493-0406

Cornell University (607) 255-2770

Museums With Expertise

Most major and medium-sized museums of every discipline have internship programs.

Colonial Williamsburg Foundation
Drawer C
Williamsburg, VA 23187
(804) 229-1000

Horner Museum
Oregon State University
Gill Coliseum L-1
Corvallis, OR 97331-4101
(503) 737-2951

Virginia Museum of Fine Arts
2800 Grove Avenue
Richmond, VA 23221-2466
(804) 367-0844

Racine County Historical Society
and Museum
701 South Main Street
Racine, WI 53403
(414) 637-8585

South Street Seaport Museum
207 Front Street
New York, NY 10038
(212) 669-9400

Written and Recorded Resources

Chase, Valerie. "Developing an Internship Program." *Current* 5 (Winter 1984): 22-23.
Suggestions for developing museum and aquarium internship programs. Includes forms, supervision, and interviewing suggestions.

Bandes, Susan J., and Selma Holo. "Intern Ins and Outs." *Museum News* 69 (July/August 1989): 54-56.

"MBA Student Groups Give Free Advice to Nonprofit Groups." *Chronicle of Philanthropy* (May 16, 1989): 17-19.

DISABLED PEOPLE AS VOLUNTEERS

Resource Organizations

See Chapter 5—Training for Special Audiences

Museums With Expertise

Museum of Science
Science Park
Boston, MA 02114-1099
(617) 589-0100
Make-up of volunteer staff includes members with physical disabilities of many types. Current survey of staff designed to evaluate attitudes, expectations and experiences working in such an integrated group, will be the basis for planned training seminars.

Oakland Museum
Education Coordinator
1000 Oak Street
Oakland, CA 94605
(510) 238-3818
Volunteer staff includes members with disabilities.

Pacific Science Center
200 Second Avenue North
Seattle, WA 98109
(206) 443-2001

Public response to blind volunteers and volunteers in wheelchairs has been very positive.

Smithsonian Institution
Accessibility Coordinator
Office of the Assistant Secretary for the Arts & Humanities
Washington, DC 20560
(202) 357-3229

Expertise in program planning, training and legal aspects of involving those with disabilities in all museum programs.

Written and Recorded Sources

Involving the Handicapped as Volunteers: A Guidebook. The Citizen Involvement for Physically Disabled Youth Project, Washington, DC: Volunteer Readership of the Points of Light Foundation, 1984.

RECRUITING A DIVERSE VOLUNTEER FORCE

USING ADVISORY GROUPS IN RECRUITMENT

Museums With Expertise

Chicago Historical Society
Clark Street at North Avenue
Chicago, IL 60614
(312) 642-4600

The society implemented a targeted recruitment plan to attract more African-American volunteers.

J. Paul Getty Museum
P.O. Box 2112
Santa Monica, CA 90407
(310) 459-7611

Increased numbers of working people participating in volunteer programs. Also

conducted informal research on staff and docent attitudes towards diversification.

Monterey County Agricultural and Rural Life Museum
P.O. Box 367
Salinas, CA 93902
(402) 755-4895

Special program where inmates from nearby correctional facility work at the museum restoring objects from the collection has increased community interest in all volunteer opportunities at the museum.

Museum of Texas Tech University
4th and Indiana
P.O. Box 4499
Lubbock, TX 79409
(806) 742-2442

Efforts to develop new relationships with previously untapped segments of its community to diversify volunteer support.

Oakland Museum
1000 Oak Street
Oakland, CA 94607-4892
(510) 238-3514

Community Guide program begun in 1990. Volunteer services manager worked with recruitment committee of community representatives from schools, service groups, council of churches, professional organizations, and charity groups to recruit for "I Dream a World" exhibition.

St. Louis Science Center
5050 Oakland Avenue
St. Louis, MO 63110
(314) 289-4400

Has developed strategies to attract members of underrepresented groups as museum volunteers.

Toledo Museum of Fine Arts
2445 Monroe Street
Toledo, OH 43620
(419) 255-8000

Conducted pilot program on multicultural recruitment.

Wing Luke Asian Museum
407 Seventh Avenue South
Seattle, WA 98104
(206) 623-5124

Multicultural perspectives in all programs, projects and exhibits, and a multicultural staff have been key to recruiting diverse volunteer force.

Written and Recorded Resources

Martinello, Marian L., and others. "Preparing Community Volunteers for Museum Education." *Curator 26* (March 1983): 37-58.

Nestor, Loretta Gutierrez. "Hispanic Americans: Tapping a New Volunteer Market." *Voluntary Action Leadership* (Fall 1984): 19-25.

Fourteen ways to increase minority involvement.

Price, William. "Smithsonian Institution's Volunteers Bring Talent and Expertise from Many Backgrounds," *The Torch* 90 (January 1990): 1.

Vineyard, Sue. *Marketing Magic for Volunteer Programs.* Downers Grove, IL: Heritage Arts, 1984.

INTERVIEWING AND PLACING VOLUNTEERS

Museums With Expertise

Buffalo Bill Historical Center
Director of Education
P.O. Box 1000
Cody, WY 82414
(307) 587-4771

Highly structured program with three levels of membership and benefits scaled to hours of service. "Interest Inventory" offers more than twenty positions including editor, curatorial aide, exhibit preparator, public relations, special events, and more.

Chicago Architecture Foundation
1800 South Prairie Avenue
Chicago, IL 60616
(213) 326-1393

Guidelines for interviewers, extensive training, evaluation of guides.

Brooklyn Botanic Garden
1000 Washington Avenue
Brooklyn, NY 11225
(718) 622-4433

Written guidelines for preparation for and conducting interviews, screening applications, and making volunteer assignments.

CHAPTER 5

Inspiring Effectiveness
Training, Professional Development, and Recognition for Volunteers

PLANNING A TRAINING CURRICULUM

Written and Recorded Resources

Volunteer manuals from the following museums and historic houses can serve as models:

The Brevard Museum of History and Natural Science, Cocoa, FL

Colorado Historical Society, Aurora, CO

Cumberland Science Museum, Nashville, TN

Denver Museum of Natural History, Denver, CO

Desert Botanical Garden, Phoenix, AZ

Hagley Museum and Library, Wilmington, DE

Henry Ford Museum and Greenfield Village, Dearborn, MI

Historic Annapolis, Annapolis, MD

Kansas State Historical Society, Kansas Museum of History, Topeka, KS

Magnolia Mound Plantation, Baton Rouge, LA

Metropolitan Museum of Art, New York, NY

National Gallery of Art, Volunteer Information Program, Washington, DC

Oakland Museum Docent Council, Oakland, CA

San Antonio Museum Association, San Antonio, TX

Smithsonian Institution, Visitor Information and Associates Reception Center, Washington, DC

South Street Seaport Museum, New York, NY

State Historical Society of North Dakota, Bismarck, ND

The Taft Museum, Cincinnati, OH

GENERAL TRAINING: COMMUNICATION

Written and Recorded Resources

Gartenhaus, Alan. "Museum Docent Dues and Don'ts." *History News* 45 (January/February 1990): 25.

The "Good Docent" Handbook, A Short Course in Techniques for Touring. San Pedro, CA: Cabrillo Marine Museum Volunteers, 1990.

Fischer, Daryl. *New Frontiers in Touring Techniques.* Denver, CO: National Docent Symposium, 1992.

Handbook developed from ideas presented at the 1992 symposium. Available from the Denver Art Museum, 100 West 14th Avenue Parkway, Denver, CO.

Grinder, Alison L., and E. Sue McCoy. *The Good Guide: A Sourcebook for Interpreters, Docents, and Tour Guides.* Scottsdale, AZ: Ironwood Press, 1985.

McDermott, Melora. *Extending Connections: A Handbook of Touring Techniques.* Oakland, CA: Oakland Museum Docent Symposium Program Committee, 1985.

Panzer, Nora. "The Docent as Catalyst." *Museologist* (Spring 1979): 9-11.

Provisional Training Manual, Weekday Volunteers, Los Angeles County Museum of Art, Museum Service Council, 1989-90.

Southerland, Margaret M. *Horticultural Volunteers: Cultivating Their Potential.* Swarthmore, PA: American Association of Botanical Gardens and Arboreta, 1980.

Tours R Us. 1990-91 Docent Training Manual. Richmond, VA: Virginia Museum of Fine Arts, 1990.

SPECIALIZED AND ADVANCED TRAINING

Applied Theatre Techniques

Resource Organizations

Free Association Theatre
5354 Etheldo Avenue
Culver City, CA 90230
(213) 390-1613

Specialized training for tours and special programs.

Douglas/Ryan Communication
2153 48th Avenue
San Francisco, CA 94116
(415) 665-6473

Workshops throughout the United States to help museum volunteers develop creativity and communications skills. Publishes *Tour Talk,* a quarterly communication newsletter for docents.

Minds in Motion Workshops
The Docent Educator
2011 Eleventh Avenue East
Seattle, WA 98102-4109
(206) 323-4966

Participatory workshops for docent training.

Museums With Expertise

Historical Society of Western Pennsylvania
4338 Bigelow Boulevard
Pittsburgh, PA 15213
(412) 681-5533

With a grant from the Junior League, the society's curator developed a training program in which volunteers researched and prepared four different scripts for tours.

Museum of Art
Rhode Island School of Design
Providence, RI 02903
(401) 331-3511

Year-long training for beginning and advanced docents including lecture series and gallery sessions. Format is designed to provide knowledge of art and history, especially as it relates to the collection and to introduce creative teaching strategies for all age groups. One of the oldest museum volunteer programs in the United States.

Utah Museum of Natural History
University of Utah
Salt Lake City, UT 84112
(801) 581-6928 or 581-4887

Optional tour presentation guidelines such as a two-minute object presentation, five-minute exhibit presentation, tour sharing, twenty- or thirty-minute theme tour, extensive docent training.

Written and Recorded Resources

Adams, Katherine. *Investing in Volunteers: A Guide to Effective Volunteer Management.* Washington, DC: National Trust for Historic Preservation, Information Series no. 37, 1985.

Agar, Julie, and others. "Docent Training Strategies within the Small Museum: a Cooperative Effort between Museum Staff and University Faculty." *Museologist* (Fall 1980): 20-21.

Bhavnani, Mitzi. "Museum Highlights Tours: Training Volunteers at the American Museum of Natural History." *Curator* 24 (September 1981): 213-20.

Carlyle, R. W. "Student Teachers as Docents: a Training Model." *Curator* (June 1988): 145-52.

Gibbons, Mary. "Volunteers: Their Recruitment, Training, Utilization and Recognition." *American Association for Museum Volunteers Newsletter* (Fall 1988).

Lowery, Lawrence F. *A Personal Training Program for Docents.* Oakland, CA: Oakland Museum, 1976.

Teaches skills to help visitors understand and interpret the contents of galleries, develop tours using these skills, and assess tour effectiveness.

Please Follow Me. Topeka, KS: Kansas Association for Museum Volunteers, KIBW-TV and the Kansas Museum of History.

Five-minute tape developed for volunteers and volunteer coordinators to illustrate teaching techniques that work best in a museum setting. Available from the Kansas Association for Museum Volunteers, Kansas Museum of History, 6425 West Sixth, Topeka, KS 66615-1099 (913) 272-8681.

"Priorities for Docent Training," *The Docent Educator* 2 (Autumn 1992): 10.

Wolins, Inez. "Teaching the Teachers." *Museum News* 69 (May/June 1990): 71-5.

Docent training program at the Pennsylvania Academy of Fine Arts.

TRAINING VOLUNTEERS TO WORK WITH SPECIAL AUDIENCES

Resource Organizations

American Foundation for the Blind
15 West 16th Street
New York, NY 10010
(212) 620-2000

Council for Exceptional Children
1920 Association Drive
Reston, VA 22019
(703) 620-3660

Friends in Art, Inc.,
of the American Council of the Blind
1629 Columbia Road, NW, Suite 800
Washington, DC 20009
(202) 667-2747

Artists, musicians, dancers, writers and actors as well as art lovers whose primary goal is making the arts more accessible by showing museums how to incorporate tactile exhibits into their collections, encouraging docents to give vivid interpretations and verbal descriptions. The organization also sponsors Voice Indexing for the Blind.

Horizons for the Blind
7001 North Clark Street, Suite 314
Chicago, IL 60626
(312) 973-7600

Consultation on access to museums for the disabled. Will advise on training docents and staff, and follow-up. Hotline to accessible places for those with disabilities: (800) 544-8646.

Museums With Expertise

These museums have conducted staff training experiences and workshops in interpretive techniques for special audiences.

Albright-Knox Art Gallery
1285 Elmwood Avenue
Buffalo, NY 14222
(716) 882-1958

The Brookfield Zoo
Special Populations Office
Chicago Zoological Society
Brookfield, IL 60513
(312) 485-0263

Museum of Science
Science Park
Boston, MA 02114-1099
(617) 589-0100

Published *Guide to Interpreting*, as manual for volunteer and staff training. Training for special needs audiences in part of regular interpreter program.

National Park Service
1100 L Street, NW
Washington, DC 20005
(202) 343-8142

Old Sturbridge Village
1 Old Sturbridge Village Road
Sturbridge, MA 01655
(508) 347-3362

Written and Recorded Resources

Groff, Gerda and Laura Gardner. *What Museum Guides Need to Know: Access for Blind and Impaired Visitors.* New York: American Foundation for the Blind, 1989.

How to greet and assist blind and visually impaired visitors. Includes training outlines, bibliography on art and museum access.

Kenney, Alice P. *Access to the Past: Museum Programs and Handicapped Visitors.* Nashville, TN: American Association for State and Local History, 1980.

Majewski, Janice. *Part of Your General Public Is Disabled, A Handbook for Guides in Museums, Zoos, and Historic Houses.* Washington, DC: Smithsonian Press, 1987.

Also contains a good bibliography and a list of national resource organizations.

Park, David C., et. al. *Interpretation for Disabled Visitors in the National Park System.* Washington, DC: National Park Service, 1984.

Trieglaff, Mark. *Brookfield Zoo's Special Populations Manual.* Chicago: Chicago Zoological Society, 1990.

Walker, Dana. *New Attitudes at the Museum.* College Park, MD: Friends in Art, American Council of the Blind, 1984.

Zorpette, G. "Sense and Sight Areas for the Visually Impaired: Museum of Folk Art in New York." *Art News* 88 (March 1989): 20.

RECOGNITION

Museums With Expertise

State Historical Society of North Dakota
North Dakota Heritage Center
Capitol Grounds
Bismarck, ND 58505
(701) 224-2674

The museum holds a yearly volunteer dinner, funded by the local Elks Club. Awards are given for work in the areas of service, achievements in hours worked, hospitality, curatorial, and behind-the-scenes. There is also a special youth award. This volunteer program has well-developed recruitment tools including job descriptions, newsletters, and brochures.

Lexington Historical Society
P.O. Box 514
Lexington, MA 02173
(617) 862-1703

Focusing on training, responsibility and rewards has led to a successful volunteer program at this museum.

Written and Recorded Resources

Vineyard, Sue. *Beyond Banquets, Plaques and Pins: Creative Ways to Recognize Volunteers and Staff.* Downers Grove, IL: Heritage Arts Publishing, 1981.

C H A P T E R 6

Communicating with One Another
Volunteer-Staff Relations

IMPROVING COMMUNICATIONS

Museums With Expertise

Detroit Institute of Arts
5200 Woodward Avenue
Detroit, MI 48202
(313) 833-7900

Extensive docent programs. A three-page guide, *Interpretation of the Roles and Responsibilities of the Staff and Volunteers,* defines working relationships.

Written and Recorded Resources

Cox, Ted. *Volunteer Program Management Guide: A Practical Manual for Planning and Managing a Science Center Volunteer Program.* Washington, DC: Association of Science-Technology Centers, 1989.

Includes a particularly useful discussion on conflict resolution.

Galley, Elizabeth B. and John R. Ogilvie. "Volunteer Committment: A Socialization Process." *Museologist* 46 (Spring, 1984): 18-22.

Dynamics of programs that succeed from the volunteers' point of view: getting in, breaking in, and settling in.

"Help Them Help You." *Museum News* 68 (March/April 1989) 60-62.

Because today's volunteers expect a return on the time they invest, negotiate volunteer service agreements with them.

Wilson, Marlene. "How to Plan for Volunteer and Staff Success." Boulder, CO: Volunteer Management Associates, (1992), audio or video cassette.

Prestwick, Patricia. "Museums, Friends, and Volunteers—A Delicate Balance." *International Journal of Museum Management and Curatorship* 2 (June 1983): 171-76.

McCurley, Steve, and Rick Lynch. *Essential Volunteer Management.* Downers Grove, IL: Heritage Arts Publishing, 1989.

Includes a chapter on volunteer/staff relations.

Nickel, Carmen Christy. *Who Am I and What Am I Doing Here? A Volunteer's View,* Tucson, AZ: Arizona Historical Society, 1987.

Report prepared as outline of issues and concerns for presentation at AASLH Annual Meeting in 1987.

Scheier, Ivan H. *Winning with Staff: A New Look at Staff Support for Volunteers.* Boulder, CO: National Information Center of Volunteerism, 1978.

Schroder, Deborah. "Can This Marriage Be Saved? Thoughts on Making the Paid Staff/Volunteer Relationship Healthier." *Voluntary Action Leadership,* Fall 1986: 16-17.

Seita, Trudy. *Leadership Skills for the Age of Nonprofits: Keeping Volunteers Happy in a Changing World.* Downers Grove, IL: Heritage Arts Publishing, 1990.

OBSERVING PROFESSIONAL PRACTICES

Written and Recorded Resources

Guidelines for Professional Practices. Detroit, MI: Detroit Institute of Arts, June 1985.
Statement of professional practices for paid staff and volunteers.

"Roles and Responsibilities of the Education Staff and Volunteers." Detroit Institute of Arts, 1988.

"Standards: A Hallmark in the Evolution of Museum Education." Standing Professional Committee on Education of the American Association of Museums. *Museum News* 69 (January/February 1990): 78-80.

Wallace, Patricia. "Volunteers Can Meet Professional Standards." *History News* 35 (June 1980): 8-9.

TRUSTEES AS VOLUNTEERS

See Section II—Trustees: Their Role in Establishing Policy

CHAPTER 7

Taking Stock

Evaluating Volunteers and the Volunteer Program

EVALUATING VOLUNTEERS AND THE VOLUNTEER PROGRAM

Museums With Expertise

Charleston Museum
360 Meeting Street
Charleston, SC 29403
(803) 722-2996

Has developed a manual to guide volunteers in conducting a self-evaluation of the volunteer program.

New York Zoological Society
185th Street & Southern Boulevard
Bronx, NY 10460
(212) 220-5141

Volunteer (Friends of the Zoo) Operating Procedures includes grievance and removal procedures.

Virginia Museum of Fine Arts
2800 Grove Avenue
Richmond, VA 23221-2466
(804) 367-0800

Docent evaluation form designed to improve quality of tour programs, identify future training needs, and identify docent's needs for additional support from the museum and school personnel. Includes self-assessment.

Valentine Museum
1015 Clay Street
Richmond, VA 23219
(804) 649-0711

The coordinator of unpaid staff, with a committee of unpaid staff evaluated the museum's volunteer program through self-study and travel to other museums with exemplary volunteer programs. A report was issued in 1990.

Written and Recorded Resources

Dean, Laurel Stulken. "Learning about Volunteer Burnout (It Can Improve Your Retention Rate)." *Voluntary Action Leadership* (Winter 1985)" 17-19.

Often the highly involved and most productive volunteer is the most vulnerable.

Hill, Donna. "How to Prevent Volunteer Burnout: An Interview with Martha Bramhall." *Voluntary Action Leadership* (Winter 1985): 20-3.

Recognition, supervision, training. Keeping rein on the overachiever.

MacKenzie, Marilyn. *Dealing with Difficult Volunteers.* Downers Grove, IL: Heritage Arts Publishing, 1988.

PUBLIC PROGRAMS

INTERPRETIVE PROGRAMS

Resource Organizations

Standing Professional Committee on Museum Education of the American Association of Museums
c/o American Association of Museums
1225 Eye Street, NW
Washington, DC 20005
(202) 289-1818

Museums With Expertise

Chicago Botanic Garden
P.O. Box 400
Glencoe, IL 60022
(708) 835-5440
At the Dr. Dissecto discovery station, costumed volunteer "nurses and doctors" assist visitors in dissecting flowers, discovering their structure and function in the process.

Conner Prairie Museum
13400 Allisonville Road
Noblesville, IN 46060-4499
(317) 776-6000
Volunteers conduct first-person and second-person interpretation during special weekend events.

Oakland Museum
Docent Council
Oakland, CA 94607
(510) 273-3514
Docent program under a board of volunteers. Team of docents and curators develop interpretive tours.

Utah Museum of Natural History
University of Utah
Salt Lake City, UT 84112
(801) 581-6928 or 581-4887
Optional tour presentation guidelines such as a two-minute object presentation, five-minute exhibit presentation, tour sharing, twenty- or thirty-minute theme tour, extensive docent training.

Written and Recorded Sources

Chadwick, Alan, and Eilean Hooper-Greenhill. "Volunteers in Museums and Galleries: A Discussion of Some of the Issues." *Museums Journal* 84 (March 1984): 177.

Cloutier, Anne. "Volunteers Unlimited." *Nature Study* 36 (March 1983): 14-15.
Educational opportunities for volunteers in zoos, museums, art galleries, and nature centers.

Gallery Instructor Program Handbook. Boston: Department of Education, Museum of Fine Arts, 1990.

McDermott, Melora. *Extending Connections: A Handbook of Touring Techniques.* Oakland, CA: Oakland Museum Docent Symposium Program Committee, 1985.

SCHOOL PROGRAMS

Resource Organizations

Museum Education Roundtable
P.O. Box 23664
Washington, DC 20026-3664
   Publishes *Journal of Museum Education* and holds workshops.

National Art Education Association
1916 Association Drive
Reston, VA 22091
(703) 860-8000
   Promotes art education in schools and museums; holds annual convention; publishes *Art Education* journal with lesson plans K-12; issues other publications.

Museums with Expertise

Asian Art Museum of San Francisco
Golden Gate Park
San Francisco, CA 94118
(415) 668-6314
   Extended School Program developed with teachers and docents, follows established curriculum guidelines for the state of California. Day-long teacher workshops.

The Folger Shakespeare Library
20 East Capitol Street, SE
Washington, DC 20003
(202) 544-4600
   Volunteers conduct educational programs for elementary and secondary school students, and activities for the general public such as readings and music concerts, and Shakespeare's Birthday Open House.

Kresge Art Museum
Michigan State University
East Lansing, MI 48824
(517) 355-7631
   Six different programs for K-6, and arts and humanities programs specifically designed to coordinate with history, English, language, social studies or art classes.

National Learning Center/
Capitol Children's Museum
800 Third Street, NE
Washington, DC 20002
(202) 675-4127
   This unique volunteer-assisted program goes beyond the traditional role of museums by conducting a full-time school for thirty-six pre-schoolers and 100 junior high school students.

North Carolina State Museum
of Natural Science
102 North Salisbury Street
Raleigh, NC 27611
(919) 733-7450
   Volunteers conduct hands-on programs with live animals and objects from museum collections to stimulate learning about the natural world.

Portland Art Museum
1219 SW Park Avenue
Portland, OR 97205
(503) 226-2811
   Volunteers conduct a program of discipline based arts education for 24,000 students in sixteen school districts, giving thirty to fifty tours per volunteer per year.

Renwick Gallery of the National
Museum of American Art
Pennsylvania Avenue & 17th Street
Washington, DC 20560
(202) 357-2700
   Explorations, Improvisation, and Lifestyles, are specialized tours and highlights

tours designed for elementary through secondary school groups.

Sterling and Francine Clark Art Institute
225 South Street
Williamstown, MA 01267
(413) 458-9545
    Volunteer docents develop and revise school tour programs.

Written and Recorded Resources

Arts to the Schools Committee Handbook, 1988-90. Detroit Institute of Arts.

Berry, Nancy and Susan Mayer. *Museum Education: History, Theory, and Practice.* Reston, VA: National Art Education Association, 1989.

Nichols, Susan K., Mary Alexander, and Ken Yellis, eds. *Museum Education Anthology-Perspectives on Informal Learning: A Decade of Roundtable Reports 1973-1983.* Washington, DC: Museum Education Roundtable, 1984.

Patterns in Practice: Selections from the Journal of Museum Education. Washington, DC: Museum Education Roundtable, 1992.

Pitman-Gelles, Bonnie, with Aubyn Kendall and Carol Bannerman. *Museums, Magic and Children: Youth Education in Museums.* Washington, DC: Association of Science-Technology Centers, 1981.

"Standards: A Hallmark in the Evolution of Museum Education." *Museum News* 69 (January/February 1990):78-80.

PROGRAMS FOR NONTRADITIONAL AUDIENCES

CULTURALLY DIVERSE AUDIENCES

Museums with Expertise

Boston Children's Museum
300 Congress Street
Boston, MA 02210
(617) 426-6500
    Has made an institution-wide commitment to culturally diverse exhibits, programming and audience development.

California Academy of Sciences
Golden Gate Park
San Francisco, CA 94118
(415) 221-5100
    Conducted focus-group interviews with their multicultural communities and developed changes based on the findings.

Maryland Science Center
601 Light Street
Baltimore, MD 21239
(301) 685-2370
    Outreach programs designed to reach new audiences.

Newark Museum
49 Washington Street
Newark, NJ 07101-0540
(201) 596-6550
    Has developed an agenda for programs to build an expanded audience.

Written and Recorded Resources

Anderson, June Maidment. "Something Special: A Museum Folk Arts Progam as Community Outreach," *Museum News* 65 (February 1986): 50-57.

Platt, Geofrey. "Ties to the Community Can Become Your Museum's Lifeline," *Museum News* 68 (May/June 1989): 33.

PROGRAMS FOR DISABLED VISITORS

Resource Organizations

See Chapter 5—Training for Special Audiences

Museums with Expertise

Oakland Museum
Services to Deaf Visitors
(Total Communications Docents)
1000 Oak Street
Oakland, CA 94607
(510) 273-3818
The San Francisco Bay area has a group of trained volunteers who sign/interpret for deaf visitors.

National Museum of American Art
8th Avenue & G Street, NW
Washington, DC 20001
(202) 357-3095
Special populations/networking information.

Orlando Museum of Art
Special Populations Programs
2416 North Mills Avenue
Orlando, Florida 32803
(407) 896-4237
Recorded information for the blind in museums.

Written and Recorded Resources

Access to Art: A Museum Directory for Blind and Visually Impaired People. New York: The Museum of Folk Art, and American Foundation for the Blind, 1989.

Feeley, Jennifer. "The Listening Eye: Tours for the Deaf in San Francisco Bay Area Museums." *Museum Studies Journal* 2 (Fall 1985): 39.

Majewski, Janice. *Part of Your General Public Is Disabled, A Handbook for Guides in Museums, Zoos, and Historic Houses.* Washington, DC: Smithsonian Institution Press, 1987.
Contains a good bibliography and a list of national resource organizations.

McGlattery, Glenn and Hartmann, Martha N. "Here Come the Touch Carts" (volunteer tactile training), *Curator* 19 (September 1986): 193-97.

Taylor, B. "A Talking Touch: The Use of Touch in Museums and Galleries by the Blind and Paritally Sighted." *Crafts* (July/August 1988): 8.

Zorpette, G. "Sense and Sight Areas for the Visually Impaired, Museum of Folk Art in New York." *Art News* 88 (March 1989): 20.

NONTRADITIONAL PROGRAMS FOR YOUTH

Museums with Expertise

Children's Museum of Houston
3201 Allen Parkway
Houston, TX 77019
(713) 522-1138
Overnight Adventures cosponsored by Junior League of Houston. Volunteers run and finance program for seven- to nine-year-old girls from economically disadvantaged families, recruited through scouting, community centers, and churches.

Fowler Museum of Cultural History
University of California
Los Angeles, CA 90024
(213) 825-4361

Trains teens from inner city to give tours of temporary exhibitions set up in neighborhood satellite museums.

New York State Museum
Education Department
CEC Building, 2nd Floor
Albany, NY 12230
(718) 473-0247
The Museum Club is an after school program designed to encourage neighborhood children to use the museum constructively through interactive learning activities in a clubhouse set among the exhibits.

OTHER PUBLIC PROGRAMS

Resource Organizations

Applied Theatre Techniques
Free Association Theatre
5354 Etheldo Avenue
Culver City, CA 90230
(213) 390-1613
Specialized training for tours and special programs.

Museums with Expertise

Morris-Jumel Mansion
160th Street & St. Nicholas Avenue
New York, NY 10032
(212) 923-8008

Minneapolis Institute of Arts
2400 Third Avenue South
Minneapolis, MN 55404
(612) 870-3203
Family Day, held one Sunday a month, is a free, thematic event centered around a special exhibition in an area of the permanent collection. Includes games, videos, special tours, storytelling, special demonstrations.

Arthur M. Sackler Gallery
1050 Independence Avenue, SW
Washington, DC 20560
(202) 357-4880
Programs such as ImaginAsia are designed to introduce kids and their parents to the museum's collections.

Written and Recorded Resources

Glasser, Susan, and David Pitman. *Artmobile Chairman's Guide.* Richmond, VA: Virginia Museum of Fine Arts.
Artmobile outreach progam takes the museum into communities.

VISITOR SERVICES

INFORMATION SERVICES

Museums With Expertise

American Museum of Natural History
Manager of Volunteers and Information
Desk Services
Central Park West & 79th Street
New York, NY 10024-5192
(212) 769-556
Services include information desk, museum highlights tours, sale of postcards and volunteer gift shop.

Los Angeles County Museum of Art
Museum Services Council
5905 Wilshire Boulevard
Los Angeles, CA 90036
(213) 857-6111
Large and efficient volunteer-administered organization.

Visitor Information and Associates
Reception Center
Smithsonian Institution
Washington, DC 20560
(202) 357-2700

Volunteers staff information desks in every museum and operate a telephone information service.

Written and Recorded Sources

Handbook: Gallery Information Committee. Gallery Information Committee, Detroit, MI: Detroit Institute of Arts, (undated).

Handbook: Volunteer Art Information Specialists. Washington DC: National Gallery of Art (undated).

Handbook for Volunteer Information Specialists. Washington, DC: Smithsonian Institution, Visitor Information and Associates Reception Center, 1991.

MUSEUM STORES AND MEMBERSHIP DESKS

Resource Organizations

Museum Store Association
501 Cherry Street, Suite 460
Denver, CO 80222
(303) 329-6968
    Sponsors conferences, and provides technical assistance for museum stores.

Museums with Expertise

Alaska State Museum
Friends Organization
395 Whittier Street
Juneau, AK 99801
(907) 465-2901
    Volunteer-managed shop.

Blithewold Gardens & Arboretum
Ferry Road
Bristol, RI 02089-0417
(401) 253-2707
    Small museum with paid shop manager. Volunteer staff recruited by the volunteer coordinator.

Cincinnati Zoo Gift Shops
3400 Vine Street
Cincinnati, OH 45220
(513) 281-4701
    Four zoo gift shops begun by volunteers, now have sales of over $1 million.

Indianapolis Museum of Art
1200 West 38th Street
Indianapolis, IN 46208
(317) 923-1331
    Volunteers staff museum shop in many jobs.

Pacific Asia Museum
46 North Los Robles Avenue
Pasadena, CA 91101
(818) 449-2742
    Volunteer committee buys and selects products under guidance of paid manager.

The Metropolitan Museum of Art
Volunteer Office
1000 Fifth Avenue
New York, NY 10028
(212) 879-5500
    Visitor Center is managed and staffed by volunteers.

Smoky Hill Museum Store
211 West Iron Avenue
Salina, KS 67402-0101
(913) 827-3958
    Small museum with shop administered by Friends of the Museum Store Committee. Volunteer manager and thirty volunteer staff.

Virginia Museum of Fine Arts
2800 Grove Avenue
Richmond, VA 23221-2466
(804) 367-0800
    Highly organized, all volunteer shop. Shop administrative volunteers, 280 sales volunteers, volunteer manager. Shop policy decisions made by a Consultation Committee.

Written and Recorded Resources

Museum Shop Handbook. The Detroit Institute of Art, Founders Society, 1988-1989.

Includes purpose and policies, training, museum contacts, organizational structure.

Museum Store Code of Ethics. Denver, CO: Museum Store Association, 1981.

Pinkston, Cynthia. "Volunteers and Museum Stores: Partners for Profit." *History News* 47 (September/October 1992): 12-16.

Williams, John C. *Retailing in the Art Gallery of Ontario.* Toronto, 1982.

An example of a business plan for a new museum shop.

Theobald, Mary Miley. *Museum Store Management.* Nashville, TN: American Association for State and Local History, 1992.

FOOD SERVICE

Museums with Expertise

Cabrillo Marine Museum
3720 Stephen White Drive
San Pedro, CA 90731
(213) 548-7562

Volunteers prepare and serve foods, act as bartenders, assist in cleanup and decorations.

Crocker Art Museum
216 O Street
Sacramento, CA 95814

Hospitality volunteers do food set-up.

Greenville County Museum of Art
420 College Street
Greenville, SC 29601
(803) 271-7570

Volunteers cook and serve for receptions and parties.

Honolulu Academy of Arts
900 South Beretania Street
Honolulu, HI 96814
(808) 538-3693

At the Garden Cafe, seventy-five volunteers help with the preparation and service of luncheons each week.

Maryland Science Center
601 Light Street
Baltimore, MD 21230
(301) 685-2370

Volunteers provide food service for members' events.

BEHIND-THE-SCENES ACTIVITIES

COLLECTIONS, EXHIBITIONS, ARCHIVES

Resource Organizations

American Association for State and Local History
172 Second Avenue North, Suite 202
Nashville, TN 37201
(615) 255-2971

Technical assistance for volunteers working with museum collections.

National Institute for Conservation
3299 K Street, NW
Washington, DC 20560
(202) 625-1495

Produces guide for emergency preparedness for museums, collection management materials, and selected bibliographies of collections care information.

Society of American Archivists
600 South Federal, Suite 504
Chicago, IL 60605
(312) 922-0140

Source for information for training volunteers to work in manuscript and photo collections.

Museums with Expertise

American Museum of Natural History
Central Park West & 79th Street
New York, NY 10024
(212) 769-5566
Specially trained teams of volunteers do archival work at the museum.

Fullerton Museum Center
301 North Pomona Avenue
Fullerton, CA 92632
(714) 738-6545
Museum has a textile and costume guild.

Georgetown Heritage Trust
Forrest-Marbury House
3350 M Street, NW
Washington, DC 20007
(202) 338-0731
Three-year-old program in which volunteers inventory the cultural and historic resources of the nation's oldest historic district, with the goal of developing the area as an ecomuseum.

Henry Ford Museum and Greenfield Village
P.O. Box 1970
Dearborn, MI 48121
(313) 271-1620
Many volunteers assist curators and conservators in projects.

Homestead Museum
15415 East Don Julian Rd.
City of Industry, CA 91745-1029
(818) 968-8492
Volunteer collections care groups clean, care for, stabilize and monitor the condition of the museum's artifacts and textiles.

Longue Vue House and Gardens
7 Bamboo Road
New Orleans, LA 70124
(504) 488-5488
Volunteers work under curator to restore textiles, maintain and restore furniture and pottery, and work on grounds.

Lynn Historical Society
125 Green Street
Lynn, MA 01902
(617) 592-2465
Ongoing volunteer projects assisting curator on photo collection.

Owls Head Transportation Museum
Route 73, P.O. Box 277
Owls Head, ME 04854
(207) 594-4418
Volunteer committees involved in vehicle maintenance.

State Historical Society of Colorado
1300 Broadway
Denver, CO 80203-2137
(303) 866-3682
Many conservators, historians, archeological, photographic, curatorial and library assistants, as well as other behind the scenes volunteers. Extensively organized, with job descriptions.

Taft Museum
316 Pike Street
Cincinnati, OH 45202
(513) 241-0343
Extensive training of volunteers for curatorial and archival work.

Written and Recorded Sources

Handbook for Volunteers Working Behind the Scenes. Washington, DC: Visitor Information and Associates Reception Center, Smithsonian Institution (undated).

Kitt, Sandra. "Forty Five Years at the Hayden Planetarium: an Archival Project." *The One-Person Library* 6 (June 1989), 1-3.

"Museum Plans Two-Week Excavation Program in Archaeology and Vertebrate Paleontology." *Lapidary Journal* 34 (May 1980): 498-500. Volunteer workers in excavation of Northwestern Illinois University and Field Museum of Natural History.

BEHIND-THE-SCENES

ADMINISTRATION, EXECUTIVE MANAGEMENT

See Chapter 4—Sources of Volunteers: Working People

Museums with Expertise

Studio Museum in Harlem
144 West 125th Street
New York, NY 10027
(212) 864-4500
    Extensive program utilizing business volunteers and retired teachers.

Smithsonian Institution
Visitor Information and Associates
Reception Center
Washington, DC 20560
(202) 357-2700
    Broad range of behind-the-scenes volunteer opportunities in Smithsonian museums and research facilities.

Written and Recorded Resources

Opportunities for Volunteer Service. Washington, DC: The Smithsonian Institution, Visitor Information and Associates Reception Center (undated).
    Lists the full range of volunteer opportunities for volunteers working on staff assistance projects.

FUND-RAISING AND SPECIAL EVENTS

Resource Organizations

Business Committee for the Arts
1775 Broadway
New York, NY 10019
(212) 664-0600
    Encourages business to support arts organizations with money, volunteer assistance, donated services and products, joint marketing, advertising, and promotional efforts.

National Society of Fund-raising Executives
15 West 72nd Street
New York, NY 10023
(212) 496-3953
    Located in most major cities, this professional association of fund-raising professionals can provide technical assistance to museums.

Museums With Expertise

Concord Museum
200 Lexington Road
Concord, MA 01742
(508) 369-9763
    Biennial flower show, "Old Concord Christmas" is major fund-raiser. Guild of Volunteers.

Old Sturbridge Village
1 Old Sturbridge Village Road
Sturbridge, MA 01566
(508) 347-3362
    Antiquarian Bookstore is major fund-raising special event.

Birmingham Botanical Gardens
2612 Lane Park Road
Birmingham, AL 35223
(205) 879-1227
    Project Committee of twelve to sixteen members is the primary fund-raising organi-

zation for the gardens, which has more than 1500 volunteers.

Friends of the Cabildo
632 Dumaine Street
New Orleans, LA 70116
(504) 568-6968

Support group stages highly successful fund-raising events such as an annual jazz festival and Halloween event. Underwrites education department and other museum activities.

Heard Museum
22 East Monte Vista Road
Phoenix, AZ 85004
(602) 257-1880

Men's Council stages the Indian Market, a highly successful fund-raising special event.

Lincoln Park Zoological Society
2200 North Cannon Drive
Chicago, IL 60614
(312) 935-6700

Renaissance Committee was formed to raise funds for major historical renovations on buildings.

Los Angeles County Museum of Art
Museum Service Council
5905 Wilshire Boulevard
Los Angeles, CA 90036
(213) 857-6101

Highly structured, totally volunteer organization. Membership Renewal Committee has had great success in using personal telephone call approach from fellow members to renew memberships.

Museum of Fine Arts
465 Huntington Avenue
Boston, MA 02115
(617) 267-9300

Art in Bloom, three-day special event is a major fund-raiser orchestrated by the museum's volunteer support group.

Nassau County Division of Museum Services
Department of Recreation and Parks
1864 Muttontown Road
Syosset, NY 11791
(516) 364-1050

Annual fair at a restored village.

Nelly's Needlers
Woodlawn Plantation
P.O. Box 36
Mt. Vernon, VA 22121
(703) 780-4000

Group of more than 100 women who conduct quilting and needlework projects that raises substantial funds in support of this historic house museum.

Society for the Preservation of New England Antiquities
Harrison Gray Otis House
141 Cambridge Street
Boston, MA 02114
(617) 227-3956

Antiquarian Bookstore and Antique Auto Show fund-raising events.

Virginia Museum of Fine Arts
2800 Grove Avenue
Richmond, VA 23221-2466

Friends of Art, a support group for members ages twenty-two to forty-five involved in fund-raising and cultural activities.

Written and Recorded Resources

Birney, Dr. Robert C. "Funding and Marketing Efforts by Volunteers." Williamsburg VA: Colonial Williamsburg Foundation, 1988.

Devney, Darcy Campion. *Organizing Special Events and Conferences A Practical Guide for Busy Volunteers and Staff.* Sarasota, FL: Pineapple Press, Inc., 1990.

A comprehensive handbook with step-by-step instructions, checklists, schedules, lists, sample budgets, and committee structure models.

COMMUNITY RELATIONS

Museums With Expertise

Museum at Drexel University
32nd & Chestnut Streets
Philadelphia, PA 19104
(215) 895-2424

Local high school and university students, sorority and fraternity members, people from the business community and individuals recruited through radio and newspaper ads helped conduct a unique Saturday morning program where children and mothers from shelters participate in arts programs designed to be culturally enriching and promote individual growth.

Virginia Museum of Fine Arts
2800 Grove Avenue
Richmond, VA 23221-2466
(804) 367-0800

Unique outreach program largely staffed by volunteers in communities throughout Virginia.

Walters Art Gallery
600 North Charles Street
Baltimore, MD 21201
(301) 547-9000

Invites people from the local community to participate with volunteers in special training on new exhibits. Members of the Jewish and Greek Orthodox community participated in a recent Jewish and Greek art exhibit.

Written and Recorded Resources

Natural Partners: How Science Centers and Community Groups Can Team Up to Increase Science Literacy. Washington, DC: Association of Science Technology Centers, July 1987.

Proceedings of a workshop on ways to increase participation of women, minorities and disabled people in science museums.

Martinello, Marian L., and Gillian E. Cook. "Training Community Volunteers for Museum Education." *Curator* 26 (March 1983): 37-58.

Platt, Geoffrey. "Ties to the Community Can Become Your Museum's Lifeline." *Museum News* 68 (May/June 1989): 33.

Pitman-Gelles, Bonnie. "Beyond Outreach: Museums and Community Organizations." *Museum News* 62 (August 1983): 36-41.

TRUSTEES: THEIR ROLE IN ESTABLISHING POLICY

Resource Organizations

Independent Sector
1828 L Street, NW
Washington, DC 20036
(202) 223-8100

Museum Trustee Association
1101 Connecticut Avenue, NW, Suite 700
Washington, DC 20036
(202) 857-1180

National Center for Nonprofit Boards
2000 L Street, NW, Suite 411
Washington, DC 20036
(202) 452-6262

Written and Recorded Resources

Discover Total Resources: A Guide for Nonprofits. Pittsburgh, PA: Mellon Bank Corporation, 1985.

A checklist of resources and techniques to help reduce an organization's vulnerability and increase its opportunities.

Ellis, Susan J., John Paul Dalsimer, and Jeffrey D. Kahn. *From the Top Down: The Executive Role in Volunteer Program Success.* Philadelphia: Energize Associates, 1986.

Hardy, James M. *Managing for Impact in Nonprofit Organizations: Corporate Planning Techniques and Applications.* Erwin, TX: Essex Press, 1984.

A Handbook for Cultural Trustees. Vancouver, BC: Canadian Museums Association (undated).

The Nonprofit Board Book: Strategies for Organizational Success. West Memphis, AR: Independent Community Consultants, Inc., 1985.

Naumer, Helmuth J. *Of Mutual Respect and Other Things: Thoughts on Museum Trusteeship.* Washington, DC: American Association of Museums, 1989.

O'Connell, Brian. *The Board Member's Book: Making a Difference in Voluntary Organizations.* New York: Foundation Center, 1985.

The Responsibilities of a Charity's Volunteer Board. Council of Better Business Bureaus, Inc. 1986.

Ullberg, Alan D., with Patricia Ullberg. *Museum Trusteeship.* Washington, DC: American Association of Museums, 1981.

Working with Volunteer Boards. Ontario: Ministry of Citizenship and Culture, 1984.

NOTES

Chapter 1

[1] American Association of Museums, *Excellence and Equity: Education and the Public Dimension of Museums* (Washington: American Association of Museums, 1992), p. 9.

[2] American Association of Museums, "Code of Ethics for Museums" (Washington: American Association of Museums, 1991), p. 4.

[3] American Association of Museums, *Data Report of the 1989 National Museum Survey* (Washington: American Association of Museums, 1992), p.86.

Chapter 2

[1] These guidelines are adapted from "Establishing a Volunteer Program: The Valentine Museum, Richmond, VA," *History News* 45, no. 1 (January/February 1990) and *Shaping the Museum: The MAP Institutional Planning Guide* (Washington: American Association of Museums, 1990). The Resource Guide lists some of the many resources available to guide the planning process.

[2] Adapted from Gerald R. Singer, "The Law: Make Sure Support Groups *Support* You, Not *Undermine* You," *Museum News* 69, no. 4 (July/August 1990), pp. 31-33.

[3] American Association of Museums, "Code of Ethics for Museums" (Washington: American Association of Museums, 1991), p. 8.

[4] Association of Art Museum Directors, *Professional Practices in Art Museums.* (New York: Association of Art Museum Directors, 1992.) p. 9. Other groups within the museum field, including educators and museum store personnel, have adopted their own statements of ethics and professional standards (see Resource Guide).

Chapter 3

[1] Office of Arts and Libraries (United Kingdom), *Volunteers in Museums and Heritage Organisations: Policy, Planning and Management* (London: HMSO, 1991), p. 36.

Chapter 4

[1] Marlene Wilson reported this information in a presentation at the annual meeting of the American Association of Museums in Denver, May 1991. A summary of her talk was published in *AAMV*, Winter 1992, p. 11.

[2] American Association of Museums, *Excellence and Equity: Education and the Public Dimension of Museums* (Washington: American Association of Museums, 1992), p. 22.

[3] A. Stellwagen, *Recruiting and Training Working People and Minorities as Docents: Report, Evaluation, and Recommendations on a Pilot Project at the Toledo Museum of Art,* Toledo, OH: Toledo Museum of Art, 1987.

[4] Adapted from Joan Crystal Pearlman and Breda Murphy Bova, "Meeting the Challenge of Diversity," *Nonprofit World* 10, no. 4 (July/August 1992), p. 22.

Chapter 7

[1] Adapted from Susan J. Ellis, "Evaluation of Volunteer Efforts," *Journal of Arts Management and Law,* Summer 1987.

ABOUT THE AMERICAN ASSOCIATION
FOR MUSEUM VOLUNTEERS

The AAMV is a national, nonprofit association representing over 375,000 volunteers in all categories of museums. The AAMV is affiliated nationally with the American Association of Museums and internationally with the World Federation of Friends of Museum.

Purpose

♦ To promote professional standards for museum volunteers

♦ To provide a forum for the exchange of ideas and information

♦ To offer opportunities for continuing education through workshops and panel discussions

♦ To encourage volunteers and volunteer managers to become familiar with volunteer projects and programs locally, nationally, and internationally

♦ To inform and represent volunteers in advocacy for tax benefits and other legislation at the local and national level

♦ To accomplish these goals in cooperation with museum directors, staff, and boards of trustees

Membership Benefits

♦ AAMV Newsletter

♦ Information on creating and sustaining a museum volunteer program and access to a network of information about volunteer projects and management

♦ Regional and state workshops focusing on volunteer issues

♦ Notification of programs on museum volunteer issues at regional, national, and international conferences

♦ Invitation to AAMV annual meeting

♦ Advocacy for benefits for museum volunteers and volunteer programs at national and local levels, both inside and outside the museum community

To Become a Member

Write to:
AAMV Administrative Office
American Association of Museums
1225 Eye Street NW
Washington, DC 20005

ABOUT THE AMERICAN COUNCIL FOR THE ARTS

Founded in 1960, the American Council for the Arts (ACA) is a national organization whose purpose is to define issues and promote public policies that advance the contributions of the arts and the artist to American life. To accomplish its mission, ACA conducts research, sponsors conferences and public forums, publishes books, reports, and periodicals, advocates before Congress for legislation that benefits the arts, and maintains a 15,000-volume specialized library. ACA is one of the nation's primary sources of legislative news affecting all of the arts and serves as a leading advisor to arts administrators, individual artists, educators, elected officials, arts patrons and the general public.

BOARD OF DIRECTORS